Greene and Cornwallis:

The Campaign in the Carolinas

For Ab and Rachael Newnam

Greene and Cornwallis:

The Campaign in the Carolinas

Hugh F. Rankin

Raleigh 1976

Table of Contents

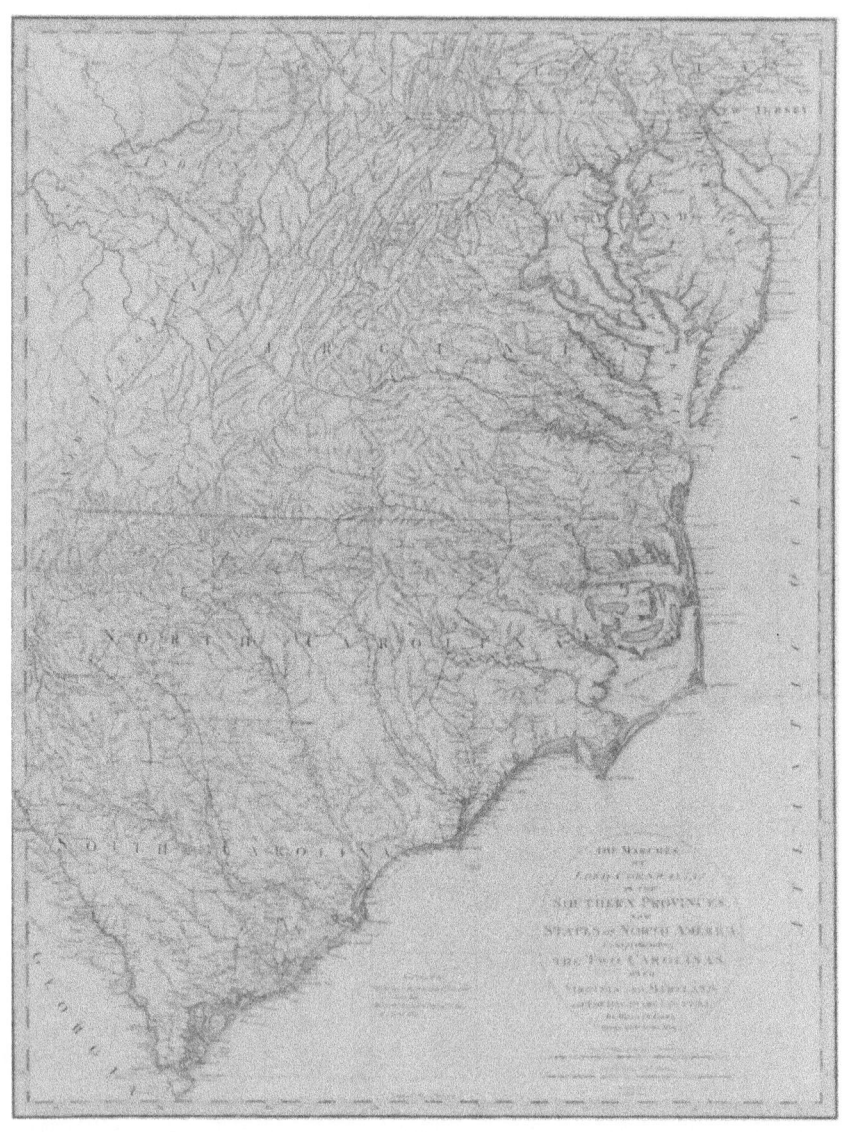

Map by William Faden, geographer to the king, 1785. Map Collection, Division of Archives and History.

CHAPTER I

GREENE COMES SOUTH

As the year 1780 drew to a close, the fortunes of war had indeed fallen low for the rebellious American colonists who had dared challenge the military might of Great Britain. Weaknesses had centered on the command function; general officers were either not living up to, or had sullied, their past reputations.

In the North, the militarily talented Benedict Arnold had almost succeeded in transferring control of the strategic post of West Point into the hands of the enemy and had thrown the Americans into a frenzy of outraged dignity and damaged pride. And to many, General George Washington and his army seemed to be doing little more than sitting around watching the enemy.

The southern states were in even more desperate straits. From the early part of 1779 the British had concentrated their primary efforts in this region because intelligence reports suggested that southerners were loyalists in sentiment and would be easier to entice back into the folds of royal allegiance. And then, too, because of the nature of its products, the area was more valuable in the scheme of British mercantilism. Moreover, it had been in this area that American generals had appeared so inept. In May, 1780, Major General Benjamin Lincoln had been forced into an inglorious surrender at Charleston. Major General Horatio Gates, successor to Lincoln and the hero of the victory over John Burgoyne at Saratoga, had indeed exchanged the "laurels of the North for the willows of the South" in the disaster at Camden, South Carolina, August 16, 1780. Charles Earl Cornwallis stood poised in South Carolina ready to strike at the rich and strategically located state of Virginia. North Carolina stood between, but that state was rather airily dismissed by British authorities as but the "road to Virginia." Only a few ragged remnants of Gates's defeated army lay between the British general and his objective.

At Hillsborough, where he had fled after the defeat at Camden, Gates was frantically attempting to reorganize his Southern Army. Members of the Continental Congress in Philadelphia who, in the not too distant past, had sent Gates south with cheers and declarations that he would "Burgoyne" Cornwallis for sure, now

1

clamored for his recall. Rumors from the Carolinas said that Gates had lost the confidence of the people and was at odds with his second-in-command, William Smallwood, who had just been promoted to major general and who was not above criticizing his commanding general. The cry for the removal of the unfortunate Gates grew louder and more persistent.

Major General Nathanael Greene of Rhode Island was the choice of many and, in some respects, the natural selection for the command of the Southern Department. He had served directly under Washington since the siege of Boston, and it was said that the commanding general had designated Greene as his successor should death strike him down before the end of the war. But Greene was by no means a unanimous choice. It was whispered that he had given Washington bad advice. Greene's pique and subsequent resignation from the post of quartermaster general on August 1, 1780, in evident disgust at the proposed reorganization of the army, had thrown Congress "into a degree of vexatious distress." And then there were those who felt that Smallwood deserved the post.

Alexander Hamilton, serving as an aide to Washington, was quick to use his facile pen to condemn Gates and beat the drum for Greene to members of Congress. In one of his letters, after heartily condemning Gates for his hasty departure from the battlefield at Camden, he added the ringing recommendation, "for God's sake, overcome prejudice and send GREENE. You know my opinion of him. I stake my reputation on the events, give him but fair play."

Congress, however, was cautious. That body had insisted upon the earlier appointment of Gates, although at the time Washington had expressed a preference for Greene. This time the responsibility was passed to the commanding general and on October 8, 1780, Congress instructed Washington to institute a court of enquiry into the conduct of General Gates and to appoint a successor until such enquiry was complete. John Mathews of the South Carolina delegation wrote Washington, "I am authorized by the Delegates of the three southern states to communicate to your Excellency their wish that Majr. Genl. Greene may be the officer appointed to the command of the southern department, if it would not be incompatible with the rules of the army."

Greene, who had just finished presiding over the board of general officers which had convicted Major John André, had his eye on another command, that so recently held by Benedict Arnold —West Point and the area east of the Hudson River. Washington

Alexander Hamilton

Horatio Gates

granted his request, but on a temporary basis. Greene felt that he was situated for the winter and sent for his vivacious wife, Catherine, whose practice it had been to visit her husband in winter quarters whenever possible.

When Washington received notice of the wishes of Congress relative to the commanding general of the Southern Department, he immediately notified Greene of his appointment with, "I wish your earliest arrival, that there be no circumstances to retard your proceedings to the southward." Greene was properly grateful for the opportunity for an independent command, but he was not too enthusiastic about the general's suggestion that he hasten to his new post, pleading that he needed time to clear up "domestic concerns," and that his health was none too good, "having had a considerable fever upon me for several days."

Washington, in his reply, left little doubt that he meant what he said about haste. Realizing this, Greene replied that he was preparing for the journey; the only disturbing thing, he said, was that he had written his wife to join him and he feared "the disappointment of not seeing me, added to the shock of my going to the southward . . . will have some disagreeable effect upon her health." And the following day he wrote Caty, "Nothing s[h]ould have torn me from you but the General's absolute orders to come on and not let anything detain me—not even ill health."

3

His friends were happy about the appointment. Major General Robert Howe, of North Carolina, who himself had served as commanding general in the South and had met misfortune in the military way, declared, "General Greene will deserve success whether he obtains it or not."

In their conference at Preakness, New York, Washington conferred far-reaching powers upon Greene. He was to be allowed to trust his own prudence and judgment in the conduct of future campaigns in the South. The fabulous Prussian, Baron von Steuben, was to be assigned to Greene's army in the capacity of inspector general and was to be given a command commensurate with his rank. Probably the concession that pleased Greene as much as anything else was the commitment of Lieutenant Colonel "Light Horse Harry" Lee and his legion to the Southern Army. This dashing and mobile unit would provide him with the nucleus of the army he hoped to build in the South. There was one unpleasant duty—his first task upon his arrival in the South was to order a court of enquiry into the conduct of General Gates at the battle of Camden with Baron Steuben to preside over a board of five general officers.

Washington also wrote letters that he hoped would prove useful. One dispatch to the president of the Continental Congress urged that body to give Greene its confidence and support for, "In the command he is going into he will have every disadvantage to struggle with." He suggested that Greene be vested with extensive powers that he might better cope with the chaotic situation then existing in the Southern Department. Soliciting aid from other members of Congress, he declared that unless something was done to strengthen the Southern Army and improve the supply situation, "the history of this war is a history of false hopes."

Lee's legion was put under marching orders, and Steuben was notified of his transfer to the South where "there is an army to be created, the mass of which is at present without any formation at all." On the following day, October 23, 1780, Greene, accompanied by two aides, Major Ichabod Burnet and Colonel Lewis Morris, along with Steuben, set out along the road to Philadelphia.

By the time he reached Philadelphia, Greene had formulated a plan through which he might be able to utilize his penchant for mobility in warfare. To Washington he reported that he envisioned a "flying army" of 800 cavalry and 1,000 infantry, to be aided occasionally by partisan forces and the militia. His primary campaign plan was to initiate harassing and nuisance raids to such an extent that the enemy would be rendered immobile and forced to defend its current positions rather than beginning new conquests. Already he had arrived at the conclusion that there was little or no prospect of raising an army capable of contesting the British army on equal terms.

He was disturbed with the reports he read of the Southern Army. The troops, he decided, were "totally unfit for any type of service. To carry them into the field in this condition, will only fill the hospitals and sacrifice the lives of many valuable men." Arms and wagons, he heard, were not so scarce as clothing.

There was little encouragement to be found in Philadelphia. He spent nine days pleading with a willing, but poverty-stricken Congress. Later he was to write of his stay in Philadelphia:

> poverty was urged as a plea, in bar to every application. They all promised fair, but I fear will do little: ability is wanting with some, and inclination with others . . . . Public credit is so totally lost, that private people will not give their aid, though they see themselves involved in common ruin.

Leaving Philadelphia, Greene, on the advice of Washington, determined to visit the governors and legislatures of each state that he passed through on his way south. Annapolis, where he arrived on November 7, was his first stop. There he appeared before the legislature, outlining his needs and urging the legislators to fill their Continental quotas and cease resting their hopes in the militia. A joint committee of the two houses interviewed him and promised all possible aid. The general asked that they provide five regiments of fully equipped and armed Continental infantry, one hundred wagons, each with four horses, along with a waggoner for each. He also requested that they provide twenty-two artificers to serve in a corps of artificers, along with £1,000 sterling for the purchase of intelligence. General Mordecai Gist of Maryland, who was in his own state recruiting for the Southern Army, was appointed quartermaster general for the state and commissioned to act as a liaison agent to forward supplies southward. Greene must have known that his requests were beyond the ability of the Marylanders to fulfill, but if he received anything at all, it would be an improvement. Shortly after his departure, the Maryland assembly voted him twelve thousand dollars "to be charged to the United States."

On his way to Richmond, Greene stopped for the night at Mount Vernon where he found Mrs. Washington in the midst of preparations to visit her husband, as was her custom, in winter quarters. Baron Steuben was not impressed with Mount Vernon. "If," said he, "Washington were not a better general than he was an architect, the affairs of America would be in a very bad condition."

In the Virginia capital the general was given an enthusiastic reception by Governor Thomas Jefferson, but he suffered disappointment with the general attitude of the Virginians and felt they were hiding behind a veil of false security and were "a lifeless and inanimate mass, without direction, or spirit to employ the means they possess, for their own security." It was soon apparent that the Virginians could offer little—the state was unable to furnish clothing for its troops already in the field. Greene summed it up with, "their ability is but small, their funds are empty and their credit low."

The general, growing weary of enthusiastic receptions and unenthusiastic support, employed scare tactics with Jefferson by emphasizing the vulnerability of Virginia's position. He reminded the governor that the original plan of the British had been to push through North Carolina and secure the lower half of Virginia. Once this was done, the enemy had only to sit tight and wait until the time of the militia had expired and then, with nothing to oppose them, they could occupy the remainder of the state with little or no resistance. He pointed out to Jefferson that opposing the enemy in the Carolinas would be less harmful to Virginia than trying to secure Virginia after those states had been overrun by the enemy. Although it soon became apparent that few supplies would be immediately forthcoming from Virginia, the general and the governor did come up with a plan that was to play a vital role in Greene's later efforts to evade Cornwallis. This was an idea to construct light portable boats that could be mounted on wheels and transported with the troops on the march.

Because of the continued presence of Major General Alexander Leslie and British troops from New York operating in Chesapeake Bay, as well as the disorganized military situation in the state, Greene appointed Steuben to be military commander in Virginia. The militia had been called out under Generals George Weedon and Peter Muhlenberg, but the situation was fluid and lacked unity. In addition to the task of whipping these occasional soldiers into some semblance of military organization and defending the state, Steuben was charged with maintaining a supply of powder from the manufacturers and lead from the mines in Fincastle County, inspecting Continental property within the state, forwarding supplies from the North to the Southern Army, repairing the large number of useless arms that Virginia had on hand, setting up a recruiting service within the state and keeping Greene supplied with fresh troops. It was a task to try even the capabilities of a Steuben.

The inability of Virginia to supply his army with wagons gave grave concern to the general. As a former quartermaster general he was well aware of the importance of transportation for the subsistence of an army. To remedy the situation partially, he planned a survey of the rivers so that they might be used for supply routes as much as possible. In Richmond he met Lieutenant Colonel Edward Carrington, a supernumerary artillery officer of the Southern Army, who had just completed a survey of the Roanoke River as a possible route of withdrawal for Gates. Greene persuaded Carrington to retrace his steps to survey the Dan River, the south fork of the Roanoke. His mission was to determine if the Dan would admit navigation to the extent that it could be connected to the upper Yadkin by means of a portage. Then, after six days in Richmond, Greene set out upon the last stage of his journey.

The continuous pleadings for adequate support, coupled with the seemingly lackadaisical attitude of the people, were beginning to get upon the general's nerves. He still brooded because he had been unable to see his wife before he left and believed she had been "rendered exceedingly unhappy at my going to the southward." As he rode deeper into the South, the increasing thoughts of the lack of success by his predecessors, the possibility of his own defeat and the consequences to his own military reputation, began to gnaw at his self-confidence. His despondency sank so deep that he expressed his fears to Washington:

> My only consolation is, that if I fail, I hope it will not be accompanied by any marks of personal disgrace. Censure and reproach ever follow the unfortunate. This I expect, if I don't succeed; . . . the ruin of my family is what hangs most heavily upon my mind. My fortune is small, and misfortune or disgrace to me must be ruin to them.

Melancholia faded into the background of his mind as he approached Hillsborough where he expected to join his army. But upon his arrival in that village he learned that Gates, after holding his shattered army under marching orders for ten days, nervously watching feints of Leslie in Virginia, had finally moved off toward Salisbury where, according to the North Carolina Board of War, there was an adequate supply of provisions.

Governor Abner Nash had also left Hillsborough. With the news that Leslie was in Virginia he had rushed off to Halifax to prepare a defense and alert the populace to possible danger. Greene was so irritated by the governor's absence that he immediately sent off a letter to Nash, reminding him that he, the general, had already provided for the defense of Virginia. He urged Nash to bend his efforts toward filling the state's quota of Continental soldiers and preparing the militia to meet Cornwallis on the southern border of North Carolina. In addition he gave Brigadier General Jethro Sumner, a Continental officer but now acting as commander of the state militia, instructions for rehabilitating the martial strength of North Carolina. It was Greene's wish that all unwilling or disabled officers be weeded from their commands, and as a means of swelling his overall manpower, that all deserters and prisoners of war who had escaped from the enemy be brought back into active service. To facilitate this, Sumner was authorized to issue pardons to all those who fell into this category and who rejoined the army. Hillsborough was designated as the rendezvous. Greene then hurried on to Salisbury only to find that Gates had moved once again, this time to Charlotte, when Cornwallis had pulled back to South Carolina and left that town open for occupation. Reports had suggested that it was not much of an army Greene was to command. He was to find that the reports, although pessimistic, had been exaggerations.

CHAPTER II

"It is new Lords, new laws."

Arriving in Charlotte December 2, 1780, Greene discovered that Gates had reviewed the situation in Salisbury and decided that it had been a mistake to allow the Board of War to persuade him that provisions were abundant in that place. With cold weather close upon him, Gates believed that Charlotte held greater possibilities as a winter quarters, despite its recent occupation by the British. After his arrival he had dispatched Brigadier General Daniel Morgan and his light troops on a foraging expedition toward Camden. The remainder of his army he had set to work building huts for shelter against the chill winds of winter.

Despite the reported ill feelings between the two, the new commander was received by the old with the utmost cordiality and respect. The general orders of December 3 carried the news of the change in command. Later in the day Greene addressed the troops and paid Gates the compliment of confirming all of his standing orders. Washington's letter approving Greene's plan for a "flying army" caught up with him at Charlotte, but it also contained the disheartening news that the requisition for additional arms for the Southern Army could not be honored because of a delay in a shipment of ordnance from France.

Later that day Morgan rode into camp with more bad news. His foraging party had pushed into South Carolina almost to the limits of Camden but had found that most of the cattle had been driven off and there was so little grain that it was hardly worth the trouble to collect it. He did advance one bit of information that was calculated to boost the morale of the army. This was the announcement of the fall of Rugeley's Fort, an outpost of Camden. It was to mark the first of many small engagements in which troops under Greene's command were to whittle away at the British military establishment in the Carolinas.

Colonel John Rugeley, a South Carolina tory leader, who stood high in the favor of the British, was the owner of a large plantation, "Clermont," some twelve miles from Camden, and was commander of loyalist militia in the district. He had secured the rank of colonel for himself and that of major for his son-in-law. On his property there was an old log barn, at one time a council chamber, but now fortified by a shallow moat and a circle of abatis which rendered the stronghold practically impregnable to small arms fire. At this time the fort held a garrison of nearly one hundred loyalist militia and new levies, their mission to protect the tories of the district. Francis, Lord Rawdon, commandant of the post at Camden, had received intelligence of Morgan's expedition and had ordered Rugeley to retire to the protection of the main garrison at Camden. But the colonel, feeling snug and secure behind his log walls, replied that since the enemy had no artillery, he was determined to defend his post to the "last extremity."

Although Rugeley's fort was on Morgan's return route to Charlotte, he had decided that it was too strong and too near Camden to risk anything like a siege. It was suggested that the cavalry under Lieutenant Colonel William Washington reconnoiter the area. So pleased with the assignment was Washington that he exercised little caution in his approach and was so noisy that by the time he reached Rugeley's the enemy had tucked themselves in behind their walls. Washington, realizing that he could not storm the place, resorted to subterfuge. Taking the trunk of a pine tree supported by three prongs, he placed it in the shadows so as to resemble a field piece. At the same time he had a number of his men dismount and crash through the underbrush so as to suggest infantry preparing for an attack.

A corporal of dragoons was sent forward under a flag to summon Rugeley to an immediate surrender. Washington's men had played their roles so well and the demand for surrender was delivered so firmly that Rugeley, without hesitation, marched out his entire garrison as prisoners of war. The exuberant Washington promoted the corporal to sergeant on the spot, burned the fort, and retired from the field without firing a shot. Although the affair bordered on the ludicruous, neither Rugeley nor Cornwallis saw humor in the incident. Not only was the surrender humiliating, but it cost Rugeley a promotion to brigadier general of militia. For Cornwallis, it meant that a number of British regulars would have to be detached from the army to maintain order in the district.

Although the affair was a tonic for American morale, Greene had little time to relish the first victory under his southern command. Facing him was the disagreeable business of the court of enquiry into the conduct of General Gates. The testimony of those officers who had been at Camden placed no blame on the general, while a council of general officers felt that there were more immediate and more important matters that took precedence over military protocol, and that a court would not only be time-consuming but impracticable at this time. Greene affirmed his belief in Gates's innocence of wrong-doing to Alexander Hamilton:

> The battle of Camden here is represented widely different from what it is to the northward. The action was short, and succeeded by a flight, when everybody took care of himself, as well officers as soldiers. The Colonel [Otho Williams] also says that General Gates would have shared little more disgrace than is common lot of the unfortunate . . . if he had halted only at the Waxhaws or Charlotte. What little incidents either give or destroy reputation.

With this unpleasant task postponed, Greene turned to the inspection and evaluation of his new command. His findings were distressing. His first night in camp had been spent with Colonel Thomas Polk, Gates's commissary general, who reported that there was no more than a three days' supply of provisions on hand and that ammunition was dangerously low. The country around Charlotte had been gleaned bare by the foraging parties of both armies, and farmers were now hiding those cattle that had been overlooked by the British army. It was by no means a pretty picture, but Polk later made the statement that Greene, on the following morning, better understood the situation than had Gates during the entire period of his command.

As one suggestion after another for solving the supply problems was brought forward, discussed, and discarded, it became clear that the only answer was to move the camp. Foraging parties reported abandoned plantations to the south, with fields of corn still standing untouched in the fields. Summoning his engineer, the Polish volunteer Colonel Thaddeus Kosciusko, Greene sent him in search of a more suitable bivouac in the neighborhood of the Peedee River.

While awaiting the engineer's return, the general made a detailed inspection of his new command. His methodical Yankee mind was distressed when it was discovered there were no records with the army. Gates, it appeared, had either been negligent in his administrative duties or had destroyed the army accounts. There was no register of supplies drawn, individual state contributions, officers commissioned, or sources of arms and ammunition. All maps had been removed from headquarters, but it was assumed they were Gates's personal property. With no records to study, Greene was left with only his observations. His findings were appalling, with his force "nothing but the shadow of an army in the midst of distress." It was little more than a ragged, undisciplined mob, using the exigencies of war as an excuse for plundering. The militia, customarily considered and used as infantry, insisted upon coming into the field on horseback, adding to the privations of a countryside already stripped bare of forage. When the militia were not plundering the countryside, they were pillaging each other. Superior officers were openly criticized for their conduct; as Greene observed, "with the militia everybody is a general."

Discipline was lax. Desertions were frequent and returns fluctuated as men came and went as they pleased, without troubling themselves with the formalities of furloughs or leaves. Greene purposely initiated a rumor that the first deserter caught would be made an example. It had little effect. When the first deserter was brought in, he was speedily tried and convicted. The entire army was drawn up to witness his execution. That night, to learn the reaction of the rank and file, officers were sent wandering about camp to overhear the talk around the campfires. One unidentified philosopher was heard to utter the laconic observation, "It is new Lords, new laws."

From the first returns Greene found that, on paper, his command numbered 2,307 men, over half of whom were militia, with only about 800 of the total properly equipped and armed for action. The greatest need was clothing, and winter was coming on. As an expedient, Greene gathered all the sheeting and osnaburg (a burlap-like cloth used for slave clothing) in Charlotte and sent them to Salisbury to be made into shirts and overalls by the women of Rowan County. As his war chest was empty, the general offered to pay the seamstresses in salt.

Although he had envisioned a "Flying army," Greene's need for horsemen was not so great that he would tolerate ill-equipped units. The plight of Major Nelson's Virginia cavalry was so desperate that the entire unit was sent home, with the general warning Governor Jefferson not to send them back until they were properly clothed and equipped.

Every spare moment was spent in writing letters, to the Continental Congress, to Washington, to Governors Nash and Jefferson, to Joseph Reed, to Alexander Hamilton, or anyone who could be solicited to use influence in securing aid for his army. The army, despite, or perhaps because of, Gates's attempts at

Nathanael Greene

reorganization, was in a ferment of inefficiency. If Greene was to realize the near perfection he had planned for his command, there was no alternative to a sweeping reorganization and the initiation of new policies more nearly conforming to his own ideas.

His first task was to remodel his administrative staff. To assist with routine duties he selected the Marylander, Colonel Otho Williams, as adjutant general. Williams had served as deputy adjutant general under Gates and possibly could supply much of the information which would have been included in the missing Gates's documents.

Within two days of his arrival Greene had dispatched a letter to Colonel Carrington, whom he had left surveying the Dan, enclosing his appointment as quartermaster general, and with instructions to select a safe supply route from the north to the Southern Army. His first assignment was the procurement of sufficient nails and tools to build one hundred batteaux for the use of the army in crossing streams. The office of commissary general had been held by Thomas Polk of North Carolina. Polk had fallen into disfavor with Gates and had since been the target of accusations by General William Smallwood of Maryland, who had charged that Polk refused to supply any but Continental troops. Polk had submitted his resignation, to become effective when he delivered the supplies he was then engaged in collecting, and declaring, "I am far too advanced in years to undergo the task and fatigue of a Commissary General."

Major Robert Forsyth had been appointed deputy commissary general for the Southern Army, as a result of a resolution by the Continental Congress, but had found it inconvenient to leave Philadelphia at this time. But Greene was unaware of the selection, and he offered the post to young William R. Davie, a colonel in the North Carolina militia who had gained some fame as a partisan leader. Davie, at the time, was attempting to recruit a mounted troop to serve with Morgan and had no real interest in the commissary. Davie suggested that he was not the one for the job in that he knew nothing about the handling of money or accounts; Greene quickly assured him that there was little to become concerned about on this score as he had not a single dollar in his military chest.

Greene was not prepared for the ominous news that came from the North. Intelligence revealed that the British were definitely going to make the South their primary theatre of action in the spring of 1781. And there was not much of an army to offer resistance. Greene's response to the information was unlike his customary methodical approach to problems. He immediately called a council of war with Generals Smallwood and Morgan, proposing that the American army take the initiative by attacking British posts before they could be strengthened by reinforcements from New York. Both Smallwood and Morgan opposed the scheme as impracticable.

The nondescript army was beginning to show some signs of rehabilitation, but a new element had crept onto the scene which threatened to shake the structure if not destroy it entirely. Dissension had surfaced among the officers, with Major General Smallwood as the leading actor. Smallwood, although a Maryland Continental officer, had, as a result of local politics, replaced Major General Richard Caswell as commanding general of the North Carolina militia and since the Camden disaster had been instrumental in persuading many of the scattered militia to return to the field. There were those, including Gates, who suspected Smallwood of starting a whispering campaign against Gates with an intention of becoming commanding general of the Southern Department.

Greene believed Smallwood had been expecting the appointment as commanding general of the Southern Department and that the selection of Greene had been a great disappointment to him. Smallwood sulked and openly stated that he would refuse to serve so long as Steuben outranked him in the Southern Army. In fact, he went so far as to propose to Greene that the general petition Congress to date his commission as major general two years forward which not only would allow him to outrank Steuben, but to succeed as commanding officer should something happen to Greene. Greene refused to even consider the proposal. On December 10, Smallwood was sent north, ostensibly to gather and forward supplies from Maryland, but in reality to put him close enough to Philadelphia to allow him to air his grievances before Congress. Pending the approval of the General Assembly, Greene appointed Brigadier General William Lee Davidson to lead the North Carolina militia.

Even as Greene struggled with the problems of reorganization, Kosciusko returned from his reconnaissance of the Peedee with a favorable report. The army was straightway placed under marching orders, but before they could move the rains came. As the steady downpour continued, Nathanael Greene made his first major decision as commander of the Southern Army—he split his force.

The larger segment he planned to lead down to the Peedee. The other division he saw as a more mobile unit, the commander of which had to be a man of special talents. Fortunately there was such a person in camp, Brigadier General Daniel Morgan. A brawling, lusty son of the frontier, Morgan had participated in the French and Indian War, Pontiac's Rebellion, and Dunmore's War, and had prospered as a frontier farmer. He was sometimes termed the "Old Waggoner" because at the age of nineteen he had served as a teamster for Braddock's army. In 1762 he had taken possession of a small grant of land near Winchester, Virginia.

Commissioned as a captain in one of the two Virginia rifle companies in June, 1775, he had marched his men 600 miles to Boston without losing a man. He had performed in an almost spectacular fashion on Benedict Arnold's march through the wilderness to Quebec, in New Jersey, and at Saratoga. He had left the army in a huff in July, 1779, in a dispute over rank, but after the Camden defeat he had cast aside his sulks and hurried south to join Gates.

Morgan's detachment was to seek out a position on the Broad River, where they were to give protection to the whigs of that section of South Carolina and "spirit up the people." He was to forage for the army of the Peedee as well as to block British efforts to gather provisions in the area. If Morgan attacked, there would be ample room in which to conduct a retreat, and if Cornwallis threw his entire army against him, Charleston would be left open to an assault by Greene. If Lord Cornwallis attempted an invasion of North Carolina, the militia of Rowan and Mecklenburg counties, termed by one British officer, "one of the most rebellious tracts in America," could slow his progress while Greene and Morgan moved in and hammered his flanks. Should this fail and should Cornwallis successfully run the gauntlet, he could be confined to a narrow line of march with Greene and the Southern Army keeping between the red column and the seacoast, thereby blocking a possible source of supplies.

All matters taken into consideration, this decision was the greatest, and most far-reaching of any made by Greene during his command of the Southern Army, and possibly of his military career. Its effects were to become important in Washington's victory at Yorktown. By this decision, Nathanael Greene shaped his own destiny.

On December 20, after eleven days of rain, the downpour stopped and the two armies slogged off in opposite directions. The march to the Peedee slowed to a muddy crawl. Although the distance was only eighty miles, the sodden army did not reach its destination until the day after Christmas. Prospects for the procurement of provisions were brighter, but Greene noted, "This is no Egypt." And to Washington he complained, "This is really making bricks without straw." He described his new bivouac as a "camp of repose; and no army ever wanted one more."

Desertions continued despite the execution of the deserter at Charlotte. Some reinforcements trickled into camp, but Greene was not overly pleased with the new arrivals. They were militia, and he loathed militia. North Carolina had maintained a great faith in the citizen solider ever since the victory over the loyalists at Moore's Creek Bridge in early 1776, a faith reinforced by the later victories at Ramsour's Mill and King's Mountain. The general constantly begged the southern states to fill their quotas in the Continental regiments, but his answer was "shoals of militia . . . who, like the locusts of Egypt, have eaten up everything, and the expense has been so enormous that it has ruined the currency of the state . . . I am convinced North Carolina has militia enough to swallow up all the revenues of America, especially under their imperfect arrangements, where every man draws and wastes as much as he pleases." As the militia were the only troops coming into camp, Greene had to discard his dream of a well-disciplined army and utilize what he had, but he concluded, "The enemy will never relinquish their plan, nor people be firm in our favor, until they behold a better barrier in the field than a voluntary militia, who are one day out, and the next, at home."

It had been Greene's intent to conduct a slashing hard-hitting kind of warfare, but he felt this to be impossible with the militia. Time was a vital factor, and to gain that time, the enemy had to be harassed and annoyed so as to throw them off balance, and kept in ignorance of future plans. To achieve this respite, the general turned to the two partisan leaders of South Carolina, Francis Marion and Thomas Sumter.

To Marion, a supernumerary Continental officer, he urged the continuation of his shifting hit and run operations. Greene wished the forest-wise followers of Marion to act as an intelligence unit, observing and reporting all movements of the enemy. They were also to function as something of a supply organization, collecting boats, rice, and other provisions as well as Negroes belonging to tories who were to be used in the housekeeping chores of the army. Greene never considered Marion's partisans to be a real fighting unit but believed them to be more of a utility unit.

A different approach was employed with the temperamental Sumter. Thomas Sumter was one who felt that warfare should be conducted to the sounds of clashing cymbals and thunder. He was also averse to authority and liked to conduct war on his own. But Sumter was a militiaman's general; as a leader of the occasional soldier he was probably unexcelled in the South. In persuading Sumter to discontinue isolated operations and bring his militia into the main army, Greene explained that, to his mind, skirmishing on the fringes of war had its place but was subordinate to the operations of the regular troops:

> The salvation of this army does not depend upon little strokes, nor should the great business of establishing a permanent army be neglected to pursue them. Partisan strokes in war are like garnishings on a table, they give splendor to the army and reputation to the officers; but they afford no substantial national security. They are matters which should not be neglected, and yet, they should not be pursued to the prejudice of more important concerns. You may strike a hundred strokes, and reap little benefit from them, unless you have a good army to take advantage of your success.

Despite Greene's settlement of the Smallwood affair, the ever-prevalent dissensions and petty jealousies among top ranking officers constantly threatened to disrupt the smooth operations of the army. Sumter, who had been wounded at Blackstocks, November 20, in an engagement with Banastre Tarleton, had become angry with Daniel Morgan, who had been so bold as to issue orders to militia officers of South Carolina without first clearing such orders with him. All of Greene's tact and persuasiveness were needed to smooth the ruffled tail feathers of the South Carolina Gamecock.

On January 9, 1781, Lee and his legion of around 280 men swaggered into camp. Lee had delayed his march to the south for several days in Philadelphia, refusing to continue until Congress supplied him with the specie, or hard money, to cover his expenses. In Richmond he had paused long enough to recruit his command to full strength.

Greene was pleased to have the crack unit with him, but the arrival of the legion meant an additional drain on an already

Francis Marion

critical supply situation. They were sent across the river to co-operate with Marion in his raids in the country between the Peedee and Santee rivers. The legion, in their natty green tunics, presented a striking contrast to Marion's ragged rabble who came and went as they pleased. Yet, despite this the two commanders were almost immediately attracted to each other. Within a short time Lee and Marion had concocted a daring raid on the coastal village of Georgetown, subject to the approval of the general. Greene had his doubts about the wisdom of such a venture, but inasmuch as the raid would have some nuisance value he gave a rather reluctant consent. The raid was unsuccessful because of the unexpected stubbornness of the British garrison. Although the foray gained nothing, it held some significance in that notice had been served on the enemy that isolated posts were subject to partisan attacks. The main army of the British would have to be weakened to strengthen such outposts if they were to be secured.

Before Lee and Marion could plan another operation, a messenger arrived from the west with earth-shaking news. Banastre Tarleton, the whip of the British army, had been defeated by Daniel Morgan!

CHAPTER III

CORNWALLIS AND THE BRITISH IN SOUTH CAROLINA

Georgia had been under British control since late December, 1778, and after the fall of Charleston in May, 1780, the two lower states in the South were supposedly once again within the British empire. To some it appeared that all the British had to do was to roll up the southern states one by one. A Rhode Island delegate to the Continental Congress observed, "it is agreed on all hands the whole state of So. Carolina hath submitted to the British government as well as Georgia. And I shall not be surprised to hear N. Carolina hath followed their example."

The British now controlled the military, economic, and political activities of South Carolina, which they were able to maintain through a chain of posts stretching westward as far as the village of Ninety-Six. Many had flocked to the King's Standard; some were those who held political opinions favorable to George III; some hoped to improve their financial status by declaring allegiance to the crown; others saw the restoration of British authority as a means of returning to that peace and tranquility they had enjoyed before the shooting started. Military rule soon destroyed their illusions. Army demands were irritating and when cattle, horses, and provisions were impressed with no promise of payment, irritation flared into anger. Displaced civil officials, some with loyalist sentiments, sulked on their plantations.

Sir Henry Clinton, commanding general of British troops in America and conqueror of Charleston, had returned to his headquarters in New York on July 5, 1780. Charles, Earl Cornwallis, had been left in command of the British army in the South. Clinton had left a pattern for the military government that he favored for South Carolina. The chief executive, according to this plan, was to be the general in command of the local government. Justice was to be administered by military tribunals. Cornwallis had sought to ease the situation by making every field officer of the loyalist militia a justice of the peace, but it became clear all too soon that they were often more severe in their judgments than regular military courts. With the British regulars and loyalist militia to execute their mandates this group soon became a power in the state, and they were especially vindictive against their former friends and neighbors who had supported the rebel cause.

After the garrison of Charleston surrendered, a number of American prisoners of war enlisted in the British army. Many of these, in turn, had deserted to the American army under Gates. Cornwallis declared that they had been joined by others who had been given their paroles and had been allowed to return to their farms. At least five prisoners had been hanged on the charge of violation of parole after the battle of Camden, having been convicted on written evidence or the testimony of slaves. During the battle proper, Lord Rawdon had crammed 160 men into the tiny jail in Camden for refusing to take up arms on the side of the British. Soon after the victory Cornwallis had sent a circular dispatch to commanders of garrisons and posts declaring:

> I have given orders that all the inhabitants of this province, who had submitted, and who have taken part in this revolt, should be punished with the greatest rigour, that they should be imprisoned, and their whole property taken from them or destroyed; I have likewise directed that compensation should be made of their effects to the persons who had been plundered and oppressed by them. I have ordered in the most positive manner, that every militia man who had bourne arms with us and had afterwards joined the enemy should be immediately hanged.

To hasten the general submission of the state, many of those prominent South Carolinians held in Charleston were offered the privilege of exchanging their paroles for oaths of allegiance to the British crown. Upon their refusal, twenty-nine of the group, including Lieutenant Governor Christopher Gadsden, were herded aboard a ship bound for St. Augustine, Florida. The general declared that this group had violated their paroles by stirring up opposition in Charleston and claimed that proof of their guilt had been discovered among the papers captured at Camden. A short time later, General Griffith Rutherford and Colonel Guion Isaacs, prisoners of war taken at Camden, were sent along with twenty-eight others to the Florida town. To the many protests Cornwallis would only answer that the measure had been "adopted from motives of policy."

Failing to suppress the whigs by threats to life and liberty, Cornwallis turned to economic repression. On September 16, 1780, he issued an order appointing John Cruden as commissioner of sequestered estates, and declaring that all property, both real and personal, of those people "acting under the authority of the rebel Congress," would be confiscated. Included were "those persons, who by an open avowal of rebellious principles, or by other notorious acts, manifested a wicked and desperate perseverance in opposing the reestablishment of his Majesty's just and lawful government." This proclamation touched many South Carolinians where threats to life and liberty had not. Many of the timid and lukewarm took the oath.

Despite fervent pleas for "Peace, peace with America," in the British House of Commons, the government endorsed the military and civil policy as established by Lord Cornwallis. Lord George Germain, secretary of state for colonies, termed it "highly judicious" and "extremely prudent and proper."

The British, and tories, once they gained the upper hand, began to act like absolute conquerors rather than benevolent rulers. Slaves were taken from prominent whigs and forced into the engineer and barrack master departments to work on fortifications and ease the housekeeping chores of the regulars.

These harsh measures, designed to force the wayward back into the fold, had the opposite effect. The whigs held the tories responsible for their persecutions and the loyalists fought back to protect their gains, remembering the years they had suffered when the whigs had the upper hand. Chafed tempers that had previously restricted the controversy to name calling and black looks were now rubbed raw and erupted into a brutal and vicious little civil war which led one latter-day British military historian to declare, "it was not the Mother Country and Colonies, but two Colonial factions that fought so savagely in Carolina." In the upper country the conflict became so savage that Lieutenant Colonel Nisbet Balfour, commandant at Ninety-Six, felt compelled to issue the order "that every man who was not in his house by a certain day, should be subject to military execution."

The imposition of such strict restrictions provided a backdrop for plundering and pillaging by both sides. The ranks of the tories swelled in proportion to British control of the state. Political principles were not always involved so much as lust for gold or political power. Greene noted this trend with, "Most people seem to be in pursuit of private gain or personal power." Many renegades gathered in small parties, roaming the countryside, terrorizing and looting the inhabitants, and always claiming fidelity to the opposite party from that of their victims. Such men were termed "Outliers" and were despised by both factions.

Soon after his arrival on the Peedee, Greene described the local scene to Alexander Hamilton:

> When I was appointed to this command, I expected to meet with many new and singular difficulties, but they infinitely exceed what I apprehended. This is really carrying on war in enemy's country; for you cannot establish the most inconsiderable magazine, or convey the smallest quantity of stores from one post to another without being obliged to detach guards for their security. The division between people is much greater than I imagined; and the whigs and tories persecute each other with savage fury. There is nothing but murder and devastation in every quarter.

The success of the loyalists was due, in large part, to the support of two British army units, although they were composed mostly of provincial recruits. The commanders of these detachments, Major James Wemyss and Lieutenant Colonel Banastre Tarleton, bore names that came to be dreaded in every whig household.

Wemyss, the lesser known of the two, was particularly active in the area of the Peedee, Lynch's River, and the Black River; he excused his activity by arguing that the people were supporting the partisans of Francis Marion. His policy of subjugation had an economic base. He placed particular emphasis on the slaughter of sheep and the destruction of looms. Those animals not killed as food for his men he ordered bayoneted. The houses of whigs and their sympathizers were burned. The torch was put to a Presbyterian church as a "house of sedition." It was reported that those suspected of rebel tendencies were given a "court-martial" before they were hanged. Wemyss's popularity with his men became evident in his attempt to surprise Sumter at Fish Dam, November 9, 1780. He had been wounded, unhorsed, and left on the field by his men to be captured by the rebels the following morning.

Wemyss had been feared and despised by the South Carolina whigs, but their special hatred was reserved for Banastre Tarleton, commanding the British Legion. They had bestowed upon him the epithet of "Bloody Tarleton." His ruthless slaughter of the Virginia troops of Colonel Abraham Buford at the Waxhaws, May 29, 1780, as they were begging for mercy, made the term "Tarleton's Quarters" synonymous with bloodshed and cruelty. The brutality of his corps at the defeat of Isaac Huger at Monck's Corner, April 14, 1780, had so enraged Major Patrick Ferguson that he had to be forcibly restrained from shooting several of Tarleton's dragoons on the spot. Tarleton allegedly made the statement "that severity

Banastre Tarleton and the British Legion

alone could effect the establishment of regal authority in America," and his actions suggest that he might well have been the author of such an opinion.

His command, the British Legion, was similar in structure to Lee's legion and wore the same green tunics. Tarleton proved as adept at house burnings as Wemyss, and he was not averse to using the hangman's noose. Upon one occasion livestock not needed as food for the British army were herded into a barn and the barn burned. The cry, "Tarleton is coming!" was enough to send the adult males of each whig family scurrying off to prepared refuges in the forests or swamps. The British position of this war on civilians was expressed in the words of one officer: "The burning of houses and the property of the inhabitants, who are our enemies, is customary in all civilized nations."

Lord Cornwallis was himself a model of contradiction. It had been this same Cornwallis who had joined with four others in the House of Lords in protesting the passage of the Declaratory Act in 1766, so long as the colonies were unrepresented in Parliament. His military exploits were both applauded and denounced in England. His victory over Gates at Camden had convinced many that he was Britain's ablest general in America, leading one of his admirers to write, "I hope you . . . will send more Troops this winter to Earl Cornwallis, who seems so well to know how to employ them." Others saw nothing but eventual ruin in his operations. One Englishman, writing to Benjamin Franklin, said, "Lord Cornwallis's military Excursion and cool Butcheries of defenceless People in South Carolina, irrevocably seals the perpetual Disunion between Great Britain and America." Horace Walpole—author, wit, and outspoken critic of Cornwallis—jibed, "The conqueror talks of severity to the late renegades; he forgets his own protests on the Stamp Act, or perhaps chooses to wash it out with blood," and later claimed that the death of John André had been "precipitated by Lord Cornwallis' cruelty."

Cornwallis had first come to America in early 1776 as a major general when he had participated in the abortive attempt against Charleston by Henry Clinton and Sir Peter Parker. He had served with distinction in the northern campaign. He had returned to England in January, 1778, recalled by the terminal illness of his wife. After her death and after his promotion to lieutenant general, he had offered to return to active duty and service in America. In his dispatch case he carried a "dormant commission," immediately elevating him to commanding general in America should anything happen to Sir Henry Clinton. He landed in New York in July, 1779, fully expecting that the home government would accept Clinton's resignation which that general had been periodically submitting since 1777. Although it had been Whitehall which refused the resignation, Cornwallis seemed to feel that it had been Clinton's fault. During the siege of Charleston word had been received that the resignation had been turned down, and from this time on Cornwallis's dispatches to Clinton took on a tone of arrogance, and his operations lent the impression that he considered his to be an independent command.

Sir Henry Clinton

After Clinton's departure from Charleston, Cornwallis seemed intent on making himself popular with his troops, even if it entailed a relaxation of discipline. The affection for him was reflected in the observation, "His army is a family, he is the father. There are no Parties, no Competitions." Banastre Tarleton was allowed to remount his legion on so many local horses that a loyalist newspaper boasted, "Colonel Tarleton took so great a number of exceeding fine horses, as enabled him to produce 400 as well mounted and well appointed cavalry as would do him credit *en revue* at Wimbleton." Soldiers were permitted to plunder almost at will. Looting was so widespread that crusty old Admiral Marriot Arbuthnot, no saint himself, earlier had felt compelled to protest, "that the province with common prudence will submit and esteem it happiness to enjoy that freedom they once possessed if Lord Cornwallis can restrain their rapacity, etc."

Lord Germain, running the war from his London office, had persuaded himself and the king that a thrust to the north with British regulars would bring out the loyalists in such numbers that the army would have little or no fighting to do and would act primarily in support of tory operations. The secretary had publicly voiced the opinion that one-half the population of America were friends of England. Cornwallis, in deference to Germain's instructions, had made contact with the North Carolina loyalists, who had, in turn, sent emissaries assuring him of their fidelity. They had also convinced the general that the response would be greater if the invasion were delayed until after the harvest was in. Cornwallis proposed that the loyalists prepare magazines or provisions to supply his army and remain quiet until the appearance of the king's troops. He, however, thought it

> difficult to form a plan of operations, which must depend so much on circumstances; but it at present appears to me, that I should endeavour to get as soon as possible to Hillsborough, and there assemble and try to arrange the friends who are inclined to arms in our favor, and endeavour to form a very large magazine for the winter, of flour, and meal from the country, and of rum, salt, etc., from Cross Creek, which I understand to be about eighty miles carriage.

Faith in the enthusiasm of the loyalists had swelled after the Camden victory. It was claimed that 1,400 tories had come into the British camp, one-half from Rowan County, considered to be a hotbed of North Carolina whiggery. Josiah Martin, the last royal governor of North Carolina, jubilantly boasted that "great proof had been given the loyalty of North Carolinians." This show of strength failed to convince Sir Henry Clinton. "It remains to be proved," he wrote Cornwallis, "whether we have friends in N.C."

The invasion to the north had been designed as a three-column thrust. Major James Craig was to command a detachment that was to assault Wilmington from the sea. Once that port was taken, the Cape Fear River could be utilized as a supply route into the interior as far as Cross Creek. The center column was to be the main army under Cornwallis. The left flank, near the mountains, was to be protected by Major Patrick Ferguson, who was recruiting loyalists in the backcountry.

In September, 1780, the army marched up to Charlotte, a village of twenty homes and a courthouse, which was to be used as a staging area from which to launch the campaign. The British had been harassed by partisan groups under the leadership of

Colonel William R. Davie, Major George Davidson, and Major Joseph Graham. Then news came out of the west that changed great expectations to frustrations. Major Ferguson, an able leader of irregular troops, had been killed, and his force had suffered a disastrous defeat at King's Mountain.

Charlotte soon became untenable. Many of the rank and file fell ill, while Cornwallis was forced to take to his bed with a "feverish cold." The partisans hampered foraging parties. The inhabitants presented such a hostile front that an aide to Cornwallis later wrote, "Charlotte is an agreeable village, but in a damned rebellious country."

The general decided to fall back into South Carolina and restructure his army of invasion and allow time for his men to recover from their illnesses. The retirement began at sunset, October 9, but their guide, William McCafferty, a Charlotte merchant, deserted them during the night. The British, panic-stricken, wandered through the darkness until daylight and then were unable to regroup fully until noon. Then, with their general suffering from every jolt of the wagon in which he lay, they hastened on to Winnsboro. Scattered along their trail they had left thirty wagons, all later taken up by the Americans. The affair at King's Mountain had not only furnished the Americans an opportunity to cheer, but it had thrown all of Cornwallis's carefully laid plans out of balance.

Sir Henry Clinton had sent a force under Major General Alexander Leslie to Portsmouth, Virginia, "the principal object of which is to make a diversion in favour of Lord Cornwallis, who, by the time you arrive there, will probably be acting in the back parts of North Carolina." To gain strength for his own army, Cornwallis wrote Leslie and ordered him to join him in South Carolina. Leslie, whose troops had been pillaging the countryside around Portsmouth, was apparently happy to comply, for he had complained to Clinton, "I am sorry to observe the Women don't Smile upon us." The transfer had been approved by Clinton, who had, in turn, ordered Brigadier General Benedict Arnold to replace Leslie in Virginia with a diversionary unit. While awaiting Leslie's arrival, Cornwallis busied himself making plans for a re-invasion of North Carolina. By late November, with his troops healthy once again, the general felt inclined to boast, "for the numbers there never was so fine an Army . . . ." And to Lord Rawdon he predicted, "we make a great change in the Southern Colonies in the next few months."

The general felt that even Greene's move down to the Peedee could be adapted to fit into his own schemes. For with the British established at Hillsborough, supplies and reinforcements from the North and destined for Greene's army could be intercepted as they moved down from Virginia. To Leslie he wrote:

> We will give our friends in North Carolina a fair trial: If they behave like men, it may be of the greatest advantage to Britain. If they are so dastardly and pusillanimous as our friends to the southward, we must leave them to their fate, and secure what we have got.

Many tories, after Ferguson's defeat at King's Mountain, had grown timid and faint of heart, which meant that the British army could not afford another loss of face. With the intelligence that Morgan had crossed the Broad River and posed a threat to Ninety-Six this problem was intensified. Ninety-Six was in an area predominantly tory in sentiment, and that post was necessary for the tories' protection. On January 1, 1781, Cornwallis dispatched Tarleton across the Broad River with a force composed of the British Legion of around 500 men and the first battalion of the 71st Regiment, their orders to bring Morgan to battle and eliminate the threat to Ninety-Six.

Tarleton found Ninety-Six to be in no immediate danger, and he halted to allow his baggage to catch up. He requested reinforcements, but the Green Dragoon was so confident of victory that he suggested that Cornwallis march the army toward King's Mountain to cut off Morgan's retreat after the forthcoming battle. The general was pleased and praised the strategy of his subordinate.

Cornwallis marched on January 7, with Leslie, who had arrived in Charleston on December 14, instructed to move out the following day. By January 17, the army had marched no farther than Turkey Creek, only thirty miles from Winnsboro and twenty-five miles south of King's Mountain, a position that would block Morgan's retreat. Cornwallis held such great confidence in Tarleton's ability that he almost hourly expected a dispatch with the news of Morgan's destruction.

Then came the news of the battle of Cowpens!

CHAPTER IV

COWPENS

Morgan had marched his detachment out of Charlotte early in the morning of December 20, 1780, and by sunset had crossed the Peedee. Within five days he had established himself across the Broad River at Grindall's Ford on the banks of the Pacolet. His command was made up of 400 Maryland Continentals and two companies of Virginia militia under Lieutenant Colonel John Eager Howard. The 100 dragoons were led by Lieutenant Colonel William Washington. Greene had directed militia leaders of the district to bring in their men to Morgan's camp as quickly as possible. Few responded. Brigadier William Lee Davidson found it difficult to call out the North Carolina militia because of a rash of Indian uprisings on the frontier. On December 28 he brought in only 120 men but almost immediately returned to North Carolina for at least 500 additional troops who he claimed were being embodied at Salisbury. Colonel Andrew Pickens arrived with sixty South Carolina militia. Other small groups drifted in, some of whom had banded together to plunder but upon hearing that Tarleton was out had come into Morgan's camp for protection.

On December 27, a patrol reported that a body of around 350 tories under a Colonel Waters had advanced into the district to a place called "Fair Forest" about twenty miles from Morgan's camp, where they were "plundering and insulting the good people of the neighborhood." Two days later 200 mounted militia under Lieutenant Colonel James McCall were added to Washington's dragoons and were sent to disperse the raiders.

With Washington's advance, the loyalists fell back some twenty miles to Hammond's Store. After a hard ride of forty miles, Washington reached the store around noon on December 30. Colonel Waters had drawn up his tories in a line along the crest of a ridge. To reach this position, Washington's horsemen had to slide down a long slope and charge up the hill. Captured pickets were persuaded to reveal the enemy's disposition of troops. Washington deployed his men. The mounted militia, with their rifles, were placed on the flanks to provide covering fire for the dragoons. On command, the militia fired and the cavalry, shouting and drawing their sabres, charged. The terrified tories fled through the trees without firing a shot, only to be ridden down by the horses or struck down by a sword. One hundred and fifty were killed and wounded while another forty were captured. Waters managed to make his escape with about sixty of his men. Washington did not lose a man. Booty collected after the battle included fifty horses and some baggage.

Forty militia under Colonel Joseph Hayes were detached to pursue the fugitives and, if possible, surprise the 125-man loyalist garrison under General Robert Cunningham in a little stockaded log hut at Williamson's plantation, within fifteen miles of Ninety-Six. Cunningham, when he heard of the approach of Hayes, hastily abandoned the post and rode hard for Ninety-Six. Hayes and his men destroyed the fort and all supplies they could not take with them. The cries of dismay from the loyalists in the district were influential in Cornwallis's conclusion that Morgan must be destroyed before he could launch his own campaign.

Morgan's force was increasing, but swelling numbers drained the community of provisions and forage. The brigadier moved his troops almost daily to make the most of limited resources. A dispatch from Greene advised him of Leslie's arrival at Charleston and carried the warning that these new arrivals might attempt to give him a "stroke." The general suggested that persons who would be unsuspected by the enemy be stationed twenty or thirty miles from camp to observe and report the progress of the British, for, "The Militia, you know, are always unsuspicious and therefore are the more easily surprised. Don't depend too much upon them." A later message emphasized Greene's confidence in Morgan's ability to deal with the situation when he warned, "Col. Tarleton is said to be on his way to pay you a visit. I doubt not he will have a decent reception and a proper dismission."

On January 16, the details left to guard the fords on the Pacolet rode into camp. Tarleton had crossed the Pacolet and was even then close on their heels. It was now obvious that Morgan, with his straggling and undisciplined militia, could retreat but little farther. He was determined, however, to choose the battle site. That morning, forcing his men to leave their food still cooking over the campfires, he marched to a place called "Hannah's Cowpens," one of the fenced spots used to mark and salt cattle by local farmers.

In the meanwhile, Tarleton had arrived at Ninety-Six and discovered that post to be under no immediate threat. He had taken this opportunity to rest his troops and send back word to "bring up my baggage, but no women." He had then written Cornwallis to suggest that the general move his army toward King's Mountain to cut off Morgan as he retreated northward before Tarleton. The general endorsed the plan: "You have done exactly what I wished you to do, and understood my intentions exactly." He reported that Tarleton's baggage was being sent on, escorted by the 71st Regiment who were to reinforce the garrison at Ninety-Six.

With this expression of confidence by his superior, Tarleton initiated a series of quick marches in pursuit of Morgan. His movements for the first few days were limited, to allow Leslie to make a junction with Cornwallis. Intelligence reported militia flocking in to join Morgan. To counterbalance this additional strength of the enemy, Tarleton requested, and received, permission to have the 71st Regiment and their three-pounder march with him. On January 14, Cornwallis wrote, "Leslie is at last out of the swamps." The tempo of the pursuit quickened. Morgan was now only six miles away.

Small detachments were ordered forward to follow closely upon Morgan's line of march. A party of tories brought in an American colonel who had wandered too far from his troops. Interrogation of the prisoner and the report of the patrol indicated that Morgan was moving in the direction of the Broad River and Thicketty Mountain. Tarleton made the decision to strike before additional men were able to come up with Morgan.

The following morning, January 17, the troops were turned out at three o'clock and marched toward Morgan's last reported position, with the baggage and its guard to follow at daybreak. It was hoped that the enemy could be surprised before they had an opportunity to form battle lines. Approaching the American camp two videttes (mounted pickets) were captured, and they reported that Morgan had halted and planned to fight at the Cowpens. Tarleton's smile broadened as his guides and the prisoners described the site. Open woods offered unlimited maneuverability for cavalry. Morgan would have to leave his flanks exposed because of the irregularities of the terrain, and the Broad River running several miles to the rear of the American position blocked an orderly withdrawal. Years after the battle Tarleton still admitted:

> The ground which General Morgan had chosen for the engagement . . . was disadvantageous for the Americans and convenient for the British. An open wood was certainly as good a place for action as Lieutenant Colonel Tarleton could desire; America does not produce many more suitable to the nature of the troops under his command.

Thicketty Mountain would have been better suited to Morgan's style of fighting, but the Broad was running deep and swift, swollen from the recent rains. To have attempted a crossing would have provided the enemy with an opportunity to catch his men while in the act of fording the muddy stream. It promised disaster, and Morgan was not a man to court misfortune.

The location selected for his stand was at the summit of a long, gently sloping ridge, where grazing cattle had cleared away the underbrush, leaving the woods open. The Broad River ran some five miles to the rear, discouraging retreat. The exposed flanks invited encirclement. It was a situation calculated to favor the army with the best cavalry, and the British Legion was acknowledged to be one of the best mounted troops in Britain's American army. Morgan later defended his choice of a site by stating:

> When men are forced to fight, they will sell their lives dearly; and I knew the dread of Tarleton's cavalry would give due weight to the protection of my bayonets. . . . Had I crossed the river, one-half of the militia would immediately have abandoned me.

His army had arrived at the Cowpens near sunset on January 16. He addressed the troops and told them of his determination to stand and fight. His words were greeted with a lusty cheer, for of late the men had heartily cursed their general for a coward, running away before the enemy. Two militia colonels by the names of Brandon and Roebuck rode in and reported that they had counted Tarleton's command as it crossed the Pacolet, and it numbered 1,150 men.

As soon as the men were comfortable, orders were issued for the militia to prepare twenty-four rounds of ammunition ready for use before they took to their blankets. The sign and countersign for the night, "Fire" and "Sword," were designed to tighten slackening spirits. Forty-five volunteers from the militia were added to Washington's cavalry. Small groups wandered in during the night, calling for arms and ammunition, relating circumstances of Tarleton's cruelty, and adding their brags to those already floating around the campfires. After a council with his officers, Morgan went out among the men. He passed among the campfires, joking with the troops and "telling them that the old waggoner would crack his whip over Ben in the morning as sure as' they lived." To the militia he cried, "Just hold up your heads, boys, three fires, and you are free, and then when you return to your homes, how the old folks will bless you, and the girls will kiss you, for your gallant conduct."

The next morning, an hour before daylight, word came that Tarleton was within five miles and marching light and fast. Morgan's voice boomed through the camp, "Boys, get up, Benny is coming." The day dawned bright and bitter cold, but the men were already moving into lines of battle.

The battleground was slightly undulating, sprinkled with red oak, hickory, and pine trees. At the crest of the long slope, Morgan placed his main line, made up of the Maryland Line, two companies of Virginia militia under Captains Triplett and Tate, with Beatty's Georgians on the right flank. The line was under the overall command of Lieutenant Colonel John Eager Howard of Maryland.

Approximately 150 yards down the slope were the militia of North Carolina, South Carolina, and Georgia under Colonel Andrew Pickens of South Carolina. Another 150 yards in front of the second line were posted 150 riflemen with Major Charles McDowell and his North Carolina backcountry men on the right and Major John Cunningham and his Georgia volunteers on the left forming a skirmish line. Colonel Washington's cavalry were positioned behind the third line, below the crest of the hill and out of the line of fire, to guard the militia horses and still be able to act in support.

Before the appearance of the enemy, Morgan rode forward to address the militiamen. In a ringing speech he assured them that he was confident that they would display their usual zeal and bravery. He exhorted them to stand firm and steady, to fire with good aim, and if they would pour in but two volleys at killing distance, he would take it upon himself to insure victory.

Riding back to the crest, he talked quietly and briefly with the seasoned men, reminding them that he had always placed confidence in their experience and courage, and assuring them that the victory was certain if they only did their part. They were warned not to become alarmed at a sudden retreat of the militia as that was all a part of his plan. When he finished speaking, he

Daniel Morgan

took his post and sat quietly on his horse, awaiting the beginning of the action.

It was near eight o'clock when the British came into view through the blue, early morning haze. Tarleton immediately deployed his tired troops, ordering them to discard all gear except their arms and ammunition. The Light Infantry, the legion infantry, and the 7th Regiment formed the main line of battle. Fifty dragoons under the command of a captain protected each flank. The 71st Regiment and the remaining dragoons were held in reserve some eighty yards in the rear. The two light artillery pieces were placed in the center of the front line.

As they moved into position the British troops were subjected to sporadic rifle fire from small groups ordered out from the skirmish line. The recruits in the 7th Regiment were nervous and threw out a scattering return fire before they were calmed by their officers. The impetuous Tarleton, exasperated with the sluggishness of his weary men, issued the order to advance before the formation was complete. As the artillery blasted forth, the infantry gave three "huzzas" and swung into a slow trot toward the American lines.

Morgan, as he galloped among his men cried out, "They give us the British halloo, boys, give them the Indian halloo, by God!"

The British advance was subjected to a "heavy and galling fire" as they drew near the skirmish line. The green and scarlet line halted, seemed to stumble and then pushed on. The first line of defense faded back through the trees, sending back an occasional shot when they found time to reload their rifles. One segment merged itself with Pickens's second line. The remainder circled around and reformed behind the third line. The British pushed forward.

As the enemy moved into range, Pickens had his men fire by regiments, thereby providing a covering fire for those who needed time to reload. The red line wavered, but discipline overcame fear and it resumed a steady advance. Then, with a lusty shout, and with empty muskets, they rushed forward in a bayonet charge. At the sight of the line of cold steel surging forward, the courage of the undisciplined militia melted within them and they began to drift to the rear. Pickens managed to retain a degree of discipline over many of his men and maintained an orderly retreat although "with haste." He reformed as many of his men as he could to the rear of the right flank of the Continentals. The remainder, panic-stricken, fled to the spot where they had left their horses.

The commander of the dragoons protecting Tarleton's right flank, a Captain Ogilvie, on seeing the flight of the militia, ordered his men to charge them. Riding among the fleeing men the dragoons became scattered and disorganized. Colonel Washington, after a hurried conference with Howard, charged the British cavalry with such force that many were toppled from their horses, unable to remount under the flashing sabres of the Americans. Those still on their horses wheeled and rode off so fast "they appeared to be as hard to stop as a drove of wild Choctaw steers, going to the Pennsylvania market."

In the meantime, the British infantry had gained confidence with the flight of the militia. Their steps quickened as they neared the final American line. They were staggered by a well directed fire. Tarleton threw in his infantry reserve, but he still did not commit his dragoons.

The British line, stretching out longer than that of the Americans, gradually began to turn the right flank. Howard, fearing an encirclement, ordered the company defending this flank to change its front. The order was mistaken, and the unit fell back. Other officers, assuming that a general retreat had been ordered, also had their men begin to withdraw. Morgan, although the retreat was orderly, rode among them, pleading for just one more volley and shouting, "Old Morgan was never beaten!"

When the general expressed his apprehensions to Howard, the colonel merely pointed to the line with the observation that men who fell back in such good order were never beaten. Morgan instructed Howard to continue his present movement until the infantry was under the protection of Washington's cavalry, while he rode back to fix a spot where the infantry were to face about and pour a sudden volley into the faces of the enemy.

It was while Howard was busying himself straightening out his line that Washington had ridden up to request permission to charge Ogilvie's dragoons. The British, seeing the Americans falling back, and thinking a rout imminent, broke ranks and rushed forward. Still Howard's line kept falling back approximately fifty yards until they reached the spot marked by Morgan. They suddenly wheeled and, at a range of ten yards, fired a volley into the faces of their astounded foe. These troops which a moment ago had been an example of British discipline and bravery, were suddenly transformed into a mass of milling, frightened individuals. Howard was quick to seize the initiative, shouting the order, "Charge bayonets!" The day was won for the Americans. Not only were the enemy thrown into a panic, throwing away their muskets and cartouche boxes, but they "did the prettiest sort of running." This sudden flight of the infantry, coinciding with Ogilvie's retreat before Washington transformed Tarleton's crack troops into a terror-stricken mob.

Morgan's men pressed forward in pursuit. There was a sudden cry of "Tarleton's Quarters," but Howard rode among the troops shouting, "Give them quarter!" Galloping among the enemy he called upon them to lay down their arms and they would receive mercy. More than 500 took advantage of the offer and surrendered. Only the artillerymen fought on, defending their pieces until they were all killed or wounded.

The British dragoons held in reserve had just been ordered to go into action when the unorthodox maneuver of the Americans had thrown the infantry back. Their precipitate retreat, in turn, threw the cavalry into confusion. Tarleton shouted orders for the horsemen to form 400 yards in the rear while he dashed forward to rally the infantry and protect his artillery.

The panic generated by the fleeing foot soldiers was communicated to the cavalry. The dragoons fled through the forest, riding down those officers who were so bold as to oppose their flight. Tarleton, screaming curses, attempted to rally his cavalry to charge the Americans, who were pushing after the British with little regard for military formation. Tarleton's horse was shot from beneath him. He caught another. Only fourteen officers and fifty men responded to his orders to reform. Without hestiation the brash young officer led them against the whole of Washington's command, and although the suddenness of his attack slowed the pursuit, "the loss sustained was in proportion to the danger of the enterprise, and the whole body was repulsed."

The struggle was fierce but short and decisive. Tradition says that Tarleton and Washington were engaged in personal combat and that Washington's horse was killed by a pistol shot from Tarleton, who is reported to have received a sword cut on the head by Washington. He turned and rode hard from the battlefield. Washington pursued. The British officer gained when Washington turned onto the wrong road and followed that for a short distance. The chase continued as far as the Pacolet. There, Washington turned back to the Cowpens.

Back on the field of battle, Morgan surveyed the scene. He had just won an overwhelming victory over a superior force with which he would have been happy to fight a draw. With a motley army of between 900 and 1,000 men he had defeated approximately 1,000 well-trained British regulars. His casualties, considering the fierceness of the battle, were amazingly light. He had lost only twelve killed and sixty wounded. By contrast, British losses were staggering. Ten officers were among the 100 killed. Prisoners of war totalled 702, including 200 wounded. Twenty-nine British officers were among the wounded. Military equipment taken included the two field pieces, two standards, 800 muskets, one traveling forge, thirty-five wagons, 100 horses and "all their musick." Also taken were seventy Negroes, brought along as servants for British officers. This amazing triumph had taken less than an hour.

It was apparent to General Morgan that although he had won the field, he could not retain possession. Cornwallis, with his entire army, would soon be marching on his trail in an attempt to recapture the prisoners and remove some of the tarnish from British military glory. A defeat would spoil the fruits of victory. Morgan decided to move at once.

Colonel Pickens was left behind with the local militia to bury the dead and collect the wounded of both armies. Approximately one day was spent at this task. The wounded were placed in captured British tents under a flag and protected by a small guard detail. Pickens then dismissed the militia and hurried after Morgan.

Morgan made no attempt to join Greene and the army on the Peedee, for Cornwallis was in such a location that he could intercept any move toward the east. To the south lay the British garrisons in the posts stretching across the state. By bearing to the northeast he could slip into North Carolina. Morgan, shortly after the end of the battle, led his men across the Broad River on past Gilbert Town. The prisoners, suspecting that Lord Cornwallis would attempt to rescue them, procrastinated. To prevent such malingering, the guards were instructed to prod them with their bayonets and they "drove the prisoners like brute beasts."

The Catawba was crossed at Sherrald's Ford. With the river as a protection Morgan pitched camp to rest his weary men. Washington, who had still been chasing Tarleton when Morgan pulled out, rode in, having crossed the Catawba at Island Ford, seventeen miles up the river. They brought twenty-six additional prisoners with them. They were herded in with the other prisoners and sent on to Salisbury, guarded by Triplett's Virginia militia whose time had expired and who were running to their homes.

On January 24, just a week after the battle, Morgan wrote Greene asking that he be allowed to resign from the army. His arthritis was acting up as a result of constant exposure in the field, and he was suffering from a severe case of hemorrhoids. His sufferings were such that he could no longer sit on his horse at a gait above a walk. He recommended that Andrew Pickens succeed him. While awaiting an answer, Morgan began making preparations to deny the passage of the river to Cornwallis.

And so was taken the first giant step on the road to Yorktown.

CHAPTER V

THE RACE TO THE DAN—Phase I

Back at the camp where Hicks Creek joined the Peedee, Nathanael Greene had concerned himself with Morgan's safety. On January 19 he had written the "Old Waggoner," cautioning him not to attempt a stand until he had numerical superiority over the enemy. He added:

> A retreat may be disagreeable, but it is not disgraceful. . . . I shall be perfectly satisfied if you keep clear of misfortune; for tho' I wish you laurels, yet I am not willing to expose the common cause to give you an opportunity to acquire them.

Even as he wrote, Morgan was in full retreat, but as a consequence of victory rather than defeat.

Major Edward Giles, Morgan's aide, rode into camp on January 23 with the exhilarating news of the Cowpens victory. The army went wild. Colonel Otho Williams, in a letter to Morgan, described the scene: "We have had a *feu de joie*, drank all your healths, swore you were the finest fellows on earth, and love you, if possible, more than ever." Within twenty-four hours Giles was sent to Philadelphia, carrying the news to the Continental Congress.

Greene's first impulse was to strike a blow at Ninety-Six to the rear of the British army, but Cornwallis was beginning to press Morgan. Word came that Morgan was moving easterly along the Catawba River, hoping to make a junction with Greene's army. Brigadier General William Lee Davidson had been requested to call out the North Carolina militia. It was Morgan's opinion that the Yadkin River offered the best defensive position. But neither the force on the Catawba nor the army of the Peedee was strong enough to offer battle to Cornwallis's entire army, especially since the latter had received reinforcements. And certainly before any contest, the two American units had to be joined.

The army of the Peedee was placed under the command of Brigadier General Isaac Huger, who had replaced Smallwood as second-in-command. Huger was ordered to march the troops to Salisbury where Greene was to join him with Morgan's men.

40

Then Greene, with a sergeant's guard of dragoons, struck off across country in search of Morgan.

Cornwallis had first learned of the Cowpens disaster from a detachment of dragoons from the British Legion who had fled into his camp. Tarleton and his group of survivors did not arrive until the following morning. An American prisoner of war who was a witness to Tarleton's report to his general said that Cornwallis was leaning on his sword as the dragoon spoke. In his fury the general pressed forward so hard that the sword broke beneath his weight, and he swore loudly that he would recover the prisoners of Cowpens, no matter what the cost.

The defeat had deprived Cornwallis of his light troops who had been destined to play a major role in his invasion plans. He could not afford to lose face a second time as "defensive measures would be certain ruin to the affairs of Britain in the Southern Colonies." He made the decision to pursue Morgan with his entire army, force him to fight, and wipe out the humiliation of Cowpens. And so was made a hasty decision to launch a campaign that was to result in the termination of major military operations on American soil.

The progress of the British army was slow. Swollen streams held their pace to a crawl. On January 25, the column reached Ramsour's Mill on the south fork of the Catawba and encamped on the hill where, on the preceding June 20, whigs and tories had attempted to settle their differences with gunpowder. It was now obvious to the general that his progress was hampered by the enormous amount of supplies and the absence of light troops to patrol out in front and on the flanks of the march. It would be dangerous to send the supplies back to his South Carolina bases because of increasing partisan activity. And he had been assured by the North Carolina loyalists that magazines of provisions would be established in the vicinity of Hillsborough. He convinced himself that he would need only enough supplies to carry him to the Yadkin River.

Under the influence of this logic, Cornwallis resolved to destroy his surplus stores. A number of men were set to work collecting flour from the surrounding countryside, the remainder burning surplus wagons and supplies. Cornwallis set the example, leading other officers in burning their surplus baggage in full view of the troops. All wagons were destroyed except those loaded with medical stores, salt, and ammunition, plus four estimated to be needed

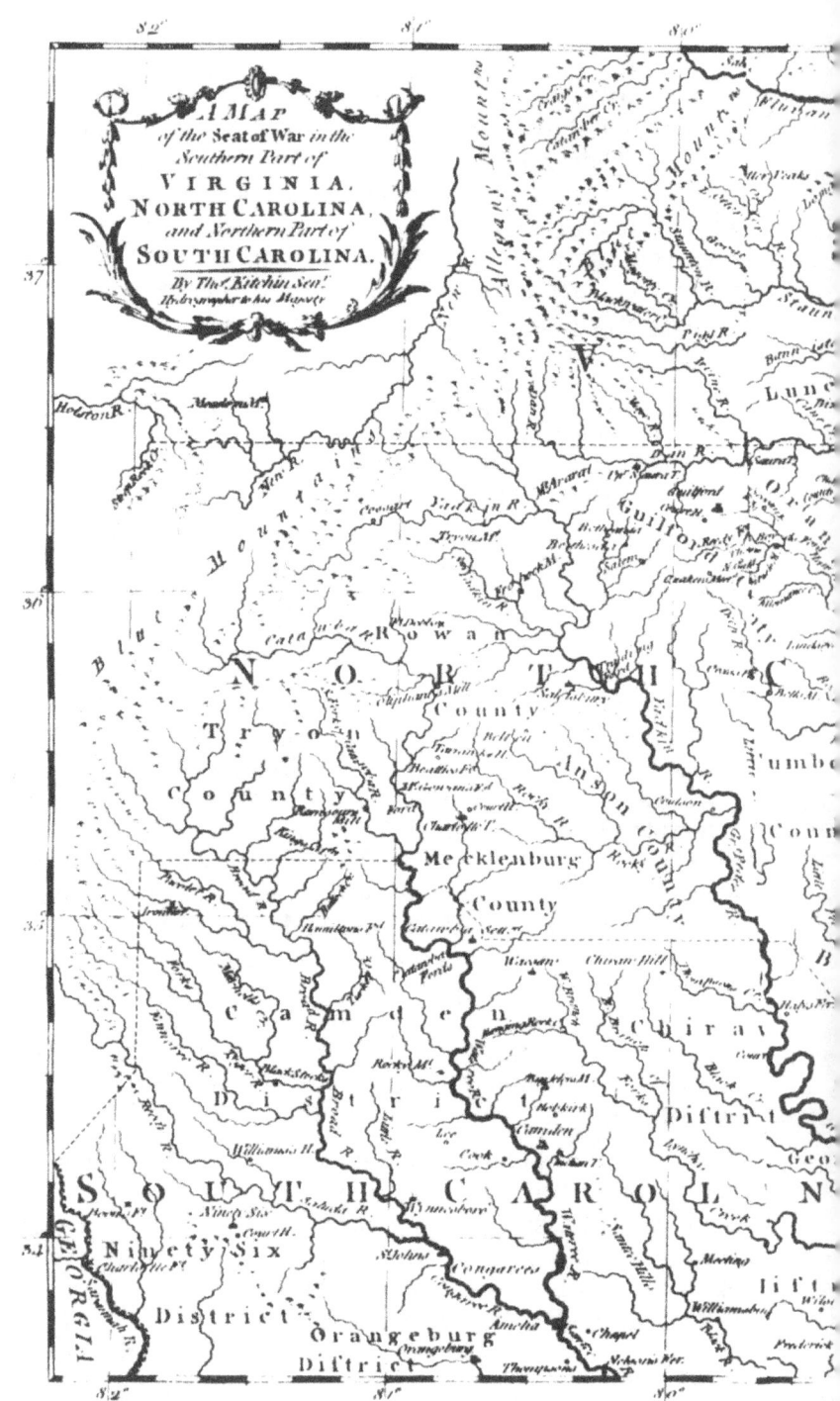

A MAP of the Seat of War in the Southern Part of VIRGINIA, NORTH CAROLINA, and Northern Part of SOUTH CAROLINA. By Thos. Kitchin Senr. Hydrographer to his Majesty

42

43

This map of the war in the South by Thomas Kitchin, Sr., first appeared in the *London Magazine* in June, 1781. Map Collection, Division of Archives and History.

for the transportation of the sick and wounded. The soldiers let out a mighty groan when all rum was poured upon the ground. Yet, in general, the rank and file accepted this as one of the hazards of war, and Cornwallis was to later note, "I must, in justice to this army, say that there was the most general and cheerful acquiescence." By the destruction of his baggage Cornwallis reasoned that he had, in a sense, compensated for the loss of his light troops at Cowpens; he had converted the entire army into light troops, encumbered only by the packs on their backs. Yet there was a flaw in his calculations—the army could march only as fast as the remaining wagons and artillery could be moved.

The halt at Ramsour's Mill, although only an interlude in a difficult campaign, became more significant with the passage of time. Sir Henry Clinton later declared that much of the failure to subdue North Carolina was the result of the action. It was his argument that the destruction of the baggage, coupled with the defeat at Cowpens, so lowered the efficiency of Cornwallis's army, that they had neither an adequate force nor ample supplies to aid the loyalists in their uprising nor protect them after they gained control.

The British approach to the Catawba was conducted in a series of short marches, designed to confuse the Americans as to the ford to be used to cross the river. The approach of the enemy, plus tales of British plunderings and atrocities in South Carolina, spread terror and consternation among the whigs of North Carolina. Many men, craving companionship in their fright, banded together to hide deep in the forest. Furniture, clothing, food, and just about every article of value was hidden, some buried and some cached in hollow trees. Horses and cattle were tethered in cane thickets or taken to the top of some high barren hill on the assumption that the British would not search in so unlikely a spot. The few schools still open were dismissed as rumors convinced many that Tarleton was ranging the countryside kidnapping young lads for service with the British army as musicians.

Before the approach of the British, the militia between the Yadkin and Catawba had been reluctant to answer a call to arms. As a sop to their indifference, General Davidson was forced to make extraordinary concessions. To enlist a troop of cavalry it was necessary to promise all those who brought their own horses, furnished their own equipment, and agreed to serve for six weeks that they would be credited with six months' service.

Still, the news of Cowpens had spurred recruiting response. Morgan had assumed the character of a giant-killer, but the general was in no condition to further his new image or direct their activities as they hoped. His old "ceatick" had returned with such intensity that he was forced to direct most of the operations from his bed. He was trying to arrange for a "chair" (a two wheeled vehicle) to transport his pain-wracked body to his home in Winchester, Virginia.

Yet Morgan did not allow pain to distract him from the task at hand. He busied himself in making plans for a defense of the river and the removal of supplies out of the path of the enemy. The prisoners and most of the stores at Salisbury were ordered to the Moravian towns, and should Cornwallis continue his push into North Carolina they were to continue on to Augusta County in Virginia. The British army was now only ten miles away, and its scouting parties were frequently spotted on the far side of the river. Several prisoners were taken, and from them it was learned that Cornwallis's immediate objective was Salisbury.

Two obscure fords, Tuckasege and Tool, were made impassable by felling trees, digging ditches, and with small detachments stationed at each. The principal ford in the area, Beatty's, was to be defended by 500 militia under General Davidson. On January 30, mounted patrols were sent to scout across the river and were chased back by enemy dragoons, but not until they had discovered that Cornwallis was now within four miles of the Catawba.

It was around two o'clock in the afternoon of January 31 when Morgan and Washington arrived to inspect the defenses at Beatty's Ford and to meet with Greene, who had sent word that he would reach the Catawba that day. Morgan had already sent his own troops marching on toward Salisbury. Within fifteen minutes of their arrival Greene rode up. After a short review of the situation with Morgan, Greene and Davidson retired to a nearby log for a council of war. As they talked, a large body of British horsemen appeared on the far side of the stream and an officer, thought to be Lord Cornwallis, repeatedly viewed the American position through a spyglass. After a twenty minute discussion, Greene rejoined Morgan and Washington and the little group cantered off toward Salisbury.

Greene's quick mind had formulated a plan of operations flexible enough to adapt to sudden changes in the military situation. He sent orders to Huger to march as quickly as possible for Salisbury, sending all surplus supplies on to Guilford Court House. A message was dispatched to Colonel James Campbell of Virginia urging that officer to join the army as expeditiously as possible with 1,000 volunteer riflemen. He hoped for a delaying action at the Catawba that would allow time for the militia to join Morgan as well as anticipated reinforcements at Salisbury to come in. If these measures should all come to pass within the next few days, Greene felt that he could force the British to do battle at a time and place of his choosing.

Shortly after Greene's departure, Davidson divided his command and led one-half off to Cowan's Ford, a private crossing some four miles down the river. The detachment at Beatty's Ford was left under the command of a Captain Farmer of the Orange County militia. On the march to the lower ford, Davidson remarked to Major Joseph Graham, commanding his nondescript cavalry, that although "General Greene had never seen the Catawba before, he appeared to know more about it than those who were raised on it." Davidson had split his force because Greene had warned that Cornwallis might attempt to cross his mounted troops by some private ford during the night so as to attack the rear of those defending Beatty's the following morning. Cowan's Ford was not reached until after darkness had fallen, and Davidson was unable to survey adequately the situation or deploy his men to take full advantage of the terrain.

On the last day of January Cornwallis had made short, almost aimless marches in an attempt to confuse American scouts, but his encampment, supposedly for the night, was nearer Cowan's than Beatty's Ford. His plan included a diversionary action. Lieutenant Colonel James Webster, a young officer of great potential, was given the command of a detachment composed of a few regulars, the baggage train, and their guard along with several artillery pieces. His mission was to create a diversion at Beatty's by a vigorous cannonade of the opposite shore while the main body attempted to force a passage at Cowan's, supposedly lightly guarded. After crossing the Catawba, the main body was to press the rear of the defenders at Beatty's.

At one o'clock in the morning British soldiers were awakened and began their march to Cowan's. Only a faint trace of a trail ran through the swamp to the ford. A three-pounder overturned and was left behind with its crew. The British column did not reach the river bank until just before daylight. Through the fog rising off the river, twinkling fires could be seen on the far shore, suggesting the strength of the defenders to be greater than anticipated. The opposite shore could not be cannonaded with a covering fire because one of the men detached to right the overturned gun had been carrying the slow match. There was no time before daylight to send for him. The waters of the river were still rising from recent rains, but the misty fog concealed the movements of the British. Cornwallis made a quick decision and ordered his men into the water, with orders not to fire until they reached the opposite bank.

A unit of light infantry, led by a tory guide, was the first into the muddy water. Each man carried his empty musket, with fixed bayonet, slung high on his left shoulder. Many carried long staves with which to brace themselves against the swirling waters. The river bottom was rocky and uneven and this, along with the rolling current, offered poor footing. Officers and men were obliged to lash themselves together to prevent being swept downstream. General Leslie's horse lost his footing and the officer was saved only by the quick thinking of an alert sergeant.

As the British reached midstream their splashings in attempts to regain their footings were heard by an American sentry, who promptly gave the alarm by firing his musket. The tory guide fled. Lieutenant Colonel Francis Hall, leading the column, not knowing that the ford sheared off at a forty-five degree angle, maintained a straight course for the shore. Davidson's men rushed to positions on the river bank and poured a "steady and galling fire" into the shadowy column stretching out toward the far shore. The British struggled on.

As the light infantry emerged dripping from the water they deployed into battle formation. Realizing that the enemy were not coming out at the regular landing, Davidson shifted his troops to dispute their landing. Graham's makeshift cavalry came lumbering up on their plough horses, but Davidson, remembering Greene's warning that the British might cross at another ford and come in on the rear, refused to commit them to action. They were stationed on a ridge some 200 yards to the rear. By this time the light infantry had managed to load their muskets and fired a volley to protect those still struggling through the water. As the British troops continued to emerge from the river and methodically form into battle formation, Davidson pulled his men back to a new position to take advantage of the dense undergrowth.

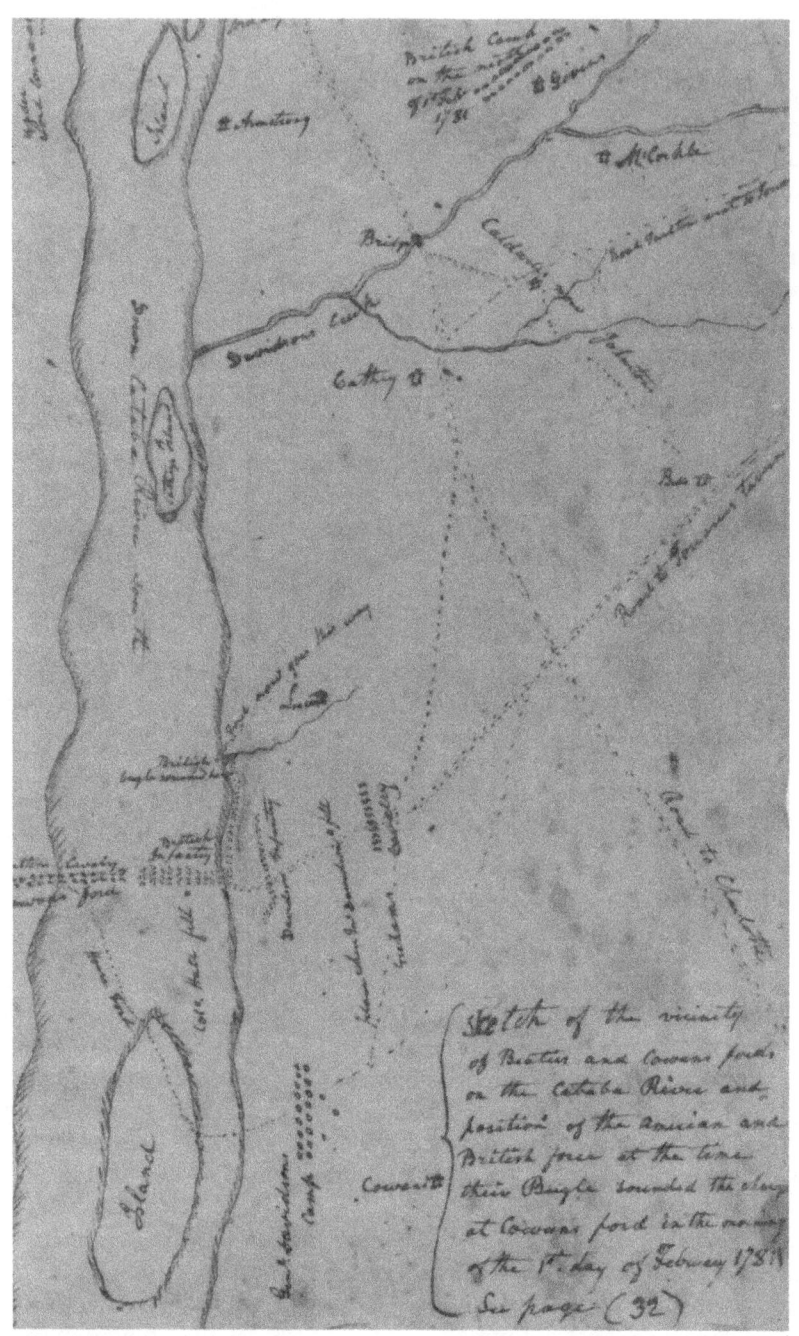

This sketch of the battle lines at Cowan's Ford is located in the Joseph Graham Papers in the State Archives. Map Collection, Division of Archives and History.

Many frightened militiamen refused to take cover and continued their drift to the rear. General Davidson, mounting his horse to rally the timid, was struck by a ball in the chest and instantly killed.

As additional British infantry straggled out of the water to furnish covering fire, the light infantry charged with fixed bayonets. The militia fled in wild disorder, making what one observer described as "straight shirt tails."

As Cornwallis sat watching his remaining troops complete the crossing, his horse, which had received a musket ball while still in the water, collapsed beneath him. The dead and wounded were collected. Cornwallis listed Lieutenant Colonel Hall and three rank and file killed. This claim was later disputed by American participants, one of whom declared at least 100 British regulars killed and that later a large number of bodies were found in the fish traps below the ford and the "river stunk with carcasses." One loss not included in casualty lists was a fine beaver hat, found ten miles down the river and marked inside "Property of Josiah Martin, Governor." Martin, the last royal governor of North Carolina, was accompanying Cornwallis in the hope of spiriting up the loyalists and in expectation of reestablishing royal government once the state was back within the fold.

With his command safely across the river, Cornwallis marched to make a junction with Webster's detachment which had experienced little resistance at Beatty's Ford.

After the uniting of the two forces, Tarleton was sent out to patrol the countryside, seeking information as to Greene's disposition of troops. A steady rain was falling and the muddy roads slowed his progress; the infantry were left about five miles from Beatty's, and he continued the patrol with only the mounted troops. From a captured militiaman he learned that the militia of Rowan and Mecklenburg counties were supposed to join the defenders of the fords at Torrance's (or Tarrant's) Tavern by two o'clock that afternoon.

The sounds of battle at the fords had set the whole country in motion, many people loading their valuables in wagons and fleeing before the advance of the enemy. A sizable number had sought the protection of the militia assembling at Torrance's. The day was raw, wet and cold, and rum was brought from the tavern by the pail full. With the appearance of Tarleton and his troops, many ran for the protection of the trees, still clutching their pails of rum. The braver of the militia prepared to make a stand.

When Tarleton came in sight of the tavern, he saw what he later claimed were over 500 militia assembling. Appealing to the emotions of his men, he recalled for them the shame of Cowpens, reminding them that here was an opportunity to erase a portion of that blot upon the record of the legion.

As the dragoons charged they were met with a sporadic and scattered fire. The sight of the swinging gray steel of cavalry sabres was too much for the militia. They ran. Tarleton reported his casualties as seven killed and wounded and a loss of twenty horses. He declared he had killed twenty of the militia, although a British officer who later rode over the ground said, "he did not see ten dead bodies of the provincials as a whole." The tavern, operated by the widow of a whig casualty of the battle of Ramsour's Mill, was burned by the main body of the British army when it passed the following day.

These two skirmishes, although relatively small, became significant in that the people of the district were too frightened to rise again until the British had crossed the Yadkin and even then they were reluctant to take the field. Greene was thereby deprived of possible replacements.

And the chase was on.

CHAPTER VI

THE HARE AND THE HOUNDS: THE RACE TO THE DAN—
Phase II

The failure of the militia to hold the fords disrupted Greene's plans. A dispatch to Huger ordered him, if he could not reach Salisbury within twenty-four hours, to change his line of march and push for Guilford Court House. Circular letters were sent to the militia leaders of North Carolina, urging them to call out their troops.

Morgan had marched his men all day and into the night of February 1. David Cain's farm, near Oliphant's Mill, had been designated as a rendezvous for the militia should the enemy force a passage of the river. Greene waited alone at Cain's until past midnight. Not a man showed. He rode on toward Salisbury.

Doctor Joseph Reed, a surgeon in Greene's army, was resting in the tavern kept by Mrs. Elizabeth Maxwell Steele, writing paroles for wounded British officers when he saw Greene ride in. After breakfast, or so the story goes, and as he was preparing to leave, Mrs. Steele gave the general her savings, two small bags of coin. Greene walked across the room to the wall where small portraits of George III and Queen Charlotte were hung. Seizing a piece of charcoal from the fireplace, he turned the picture of the king to the wall and scrawled across the back, "O George hide thy face and mourn."

While supervising the removal of the stores from Salisbury, the general was distressed to discover that nearly 1,700 muskets, collected in that town for the use of the militia, had been so poorly stored that they were rusted beyond use. "These are some of the happy effects," he complained, "of defending the Country with Militia from which the good Lord deliver us."

Cornwallis moved away from the Catawba on February 2, marching along the road for Salisbury. His movement was hampered by the penchant of his troops to plunder and pillage. The smoke of burning houses traced the British line of march. That night, strongly worded orders denounced such behavior as a "Disgrace to the Army" and promised severe punishment for such future action.

When he reached Salisbury the following day, Cornwallis was informed that Morgan was at Trading Ford but had not yet crossed the Yadkin. Brigadier General Charles O'Hara was given the command of a detachment with orders to prevent Morgan from crossing the river. Rain, muddy roads, darkness, and fatigue all so slowed the movement that the British unit did not reach the Yadkin until midnight. As they approached the stream, they were greeted with a brief flurry of rifle fire. From a prisoner it was learned that the opposition had been furnished by a small detail left to guard the wagons of the "country people," fleeing before the invaders. He also provided the information that Morgan had forded the river with his wagons and horses, while crossing his men in flat boats. These flats were now tied up to the opposite shore. At daybreak, O'Hara surveyed the situation. An attempt to ford the swollen river would be dangerous, especially since Morgan's men might by laying in ambush on the far side. Artillery was rolled forward to subject Morgan's suspected position to a vigorous bombardment. O'Hara marched his infantry back to a ridge commanding the ford and sent his cavalry back to Salisbury with the word that Morgan had crossed the Yadkin.

It was this information that led Cornwallis to decide to strike for the shallow upper fords to eliminate further delays by swollen streams. Tarleton was sent to reconnoiter the upper Yadkin. At Grant's Creek he was opposed by 100 militia under Colonel Francis Locke, who had been engaged in destroying the bridge at that place. For approximately three hours this stubborn group refused Tarleton a passage of the stream. Leaving the infantry to engage the attention of the militia, Tarleton led the cavalry upstream where they crossed over to come in on the rear of the defenders. As soon as Locke noticed their absence he gave the order to retreat. The militia fled through the trees, pursued by the dragoons. Despite the length of the skirmish, there was only one casualty, one Wilson, a militiaman who was wounded as he ran through the forest. After a patrol to the shallow fords, Tarleton sent back word to Cornwallis that the way was clear. O'Hara was recalled and the British army marched up the river where they crossed over into the Moravian towns around Salem.

It now appeared to Greene that it was going to be impossible to unite Morgan's command with the army of the Peedee. Yet he believed that an attack on his forces by the British was inevitable, and he wrote Huger, "If Ld. Cornwallis knows his true interest he will pursue our army. If he can disperse that, he completes the reduction of the State, and without that, he can do nothing to effect." On February 4, the army marched, trudging over muddy roads cut into ruts by the wheels of the wagons belonging to the inhabitants flying before the advance of the British army.

The end of the first day's march found the American army at Abbot's Meeting House, and the following morning they moved on to Guilford Court House. Greene had long favored that place as a rendezvous in the event of a retreat or as a battleground if forced to fight. There was some information that the militia were beginning to assemble. Greene sent instructions to local commanders to hold their men ready to march at a moment's notice and have them bring five days' provisions with them into the field.

On February 8, there was intelligence that Cornwallis had marched for the upper Yadkin. Greene went into action. The militia were ordered to march night and day for Guilford Court House. The hospital unit and all surplus stores were sent to safety across the Dan River. All usable arms, ammunition, and flints were to be rushed to the court house for the use of those militia without arms.

The following day, February 9, Huger's tattered army, accompanied by Lee's legion, straggled into Guilford Court House. Although numerical strength had been added, there was little increase in combat effectiveness. The march from the Peedee had been marked by adversity because of "nakedness, the want of provisions, poor horses, broken harness, and bad roads." Many of the men were without shoes and their feet, cut by the frozen ridges in the roads, left bloody trails behind them.

Greene called a council of war. The wretched condition of the army of the Peedee and the failure of the militia to turn out in force ruled out any immediate action. Daily desertions sapped the army of its strength. One militia unit of 300 men shrank to thirty-six within a week, many carrying off their muskets which were of Continental issue. The American force now numbered approximately 2,000 men, while that of Cornwallis was estimated to be 3,500 well-trained soldiers.

Notwithstanding the weakened condition of his army, Greene was overpowered by a spirit of optimism and wanted to fight. He feared a continued retreat would prove disheartening to the people of the Carolinas and Virginia. But his subordinates discouraged rash actions and persuaded the general to extend his withdrawal to the far side of the Dan.

But now Cornwallis was within twenty-five miles of Guilford Court House and as near the upper crossings of the Dan as Greene! Lieutenant Colonel Carrington, who had just rejoined the army after his survey of the rivers, suggested that a passage of the Dan could be accomplished by utilizing Irwin's and Boyd's ferries on the lower part of the river. Although the stream was too deep for fording, the ferries were only five miles apart, and the boats of Dix's Ferry, twenty miles up-stream, could be floated down for use in the operation. Carrington, with a small detachment of men, was sent off to assemble the available boats.

To provide cover for his retreat, Greene formed a light force. For cavalry he detached the mounted militia and added the 240 dragoons of Lee's legion. Lieutenant Colonel John Eager Howard was given the command of 280 select infantry, sixty Virginia riflemen, and the infantry of Lee's legion. Greene offered the overall command to Morgan, but that brigadier, in addition to his sciatica, had developed such a severe case of piles that it was no longer possible for him to sit on his horse. Despite the entreaties of Greene, Morgan left the army to make his way home. The command was given to Colonel Otho H. Williams.

After sending dispatches requesting reinforcements, Greene on February 9 put his army in motion toward Virginia, leaving the light unit on the ground. Williams decamped the following day and moved to a position to intercept the British line of march.

Lord Cornwallis tarried in the Moravian towns long enough to replenish his provisions as the Moravians "were always reputed loyal." Bread and meal were supplied by these "mild and hospitable inhabitants." The hospitality extended by these gentle folk was not reciprocated, for the campfollowers and tory hangers-on stole everything possible from their benefactors.

From loyalist informants Cornwallis learned that the fords of the lower Dan were too deep for fording and could only be crossed by ferry, especially during the winter months; and he had been assured that there were not enough boats at the lower ferries to cross even a small army. As a result of this intelligence the British general moved toward the shallow upper fords of the Dan, hoping to force Greene to a decisive battle before reinforcements could arrive from Virginia.

The first contact with the Americans came when the British point engaged Williams's troops. This slowed British progress, for it became necessary for the British general to close his files before moving forward to dislodge the force obstructing his movement.

As Cornwallis probed the defense with patrols, Williams pulled out, having completed his scheme of delaying his lordship's progress for several hours. The result of this maneuver was that Cornwallis was forced to slow his march, as the constant threat of ambush obliged him to regulate his pace to that of the slowest unit. Williams moved obliquely to the northeast and continued on an intermediate road between the American and British armies. This route placed his light corps in a position with the British on his left and to the rear and the Americans to the right and front, a station calculated to intercept a move toward Greene.

Williams marched fast. His men were on the move by three o'clock every morning. As his infantry slept the mounted troops patrolled, in shifts, to guard against a surprise attack. Time was allowed for one meal each day—breakfast.

These moves convinced Cornwallis that Greene was heading for Dix's Ferry, in reality twenty miles upstream from the American goal. With this in mind, the British general crossed over to the road leading to that place, which happened to be the same path along which Williams was moving. Early in the morning of February 13, while the men were eating breakfast, a farmer rode into Colonel Williams's camp with the information that he had just seen the British on the trail only four miles to the rear. To confirm this intelligence, Lee, leading a detachment of his dragoons, was sent to investigate. The point of the enemy vanguard was engaged, and a running fight developed, in which the ebullient Lee claimed his men killed eighteen and captured several of the enemy while losing only one of his command—the young bugler.

Williams, feeling that Greene had been allowed ample time to cross the Dan, and with Cornwallis hot on his heels, struck directly for Irwin's Ferry. Lee's legion, acting as a rear guard, were involved in a number of sharp skirmishes, but because of their better mounts, managed to gain the protection of Williams's main body with no casualties. Cornwallis was pushing his men unmercifully and was soon so near that the British vanguard was often in sight of the American rear guard.

The weary Americans marched through the cold, gray February afternoon until after dark. A feeling of dismay fell over them as the glowing lights of many campfires could be seen through the shadows cast by the trees. These could only be the fires of Greene's camp, and there was the vexing thought that the light army had led the enemy to the very troops they were supposed to protect! Their anxiety faded when it was discovered that although these were indeed the fires of Greene's army, they were at least twenty-four hours old.

The march continued into the night until it became certain that the British had camped for the night. There was little time to sleep. Around midnight there were scattered firings around the pickets. Williams roused his sleepy men and resumed his advance to the river. Around noon on the following day, February 14, 1781, a messenger arrived with the welcome information that Greene was safely across the river. Williams accelerated his pace and pressed for Boyd's Ferry and late that afternoon, reached the river. Between eight and nine o'clock that night Lee's mounted troops, still acting as a rear guard, were ferried across the river. Colonel Carrington crossed over in the last boat with Lee.

Cornwallis had lost the race, a race that had endured for almost a month, and whose course was the breadth of North Carolina. Frustrated, he reviewed his situation. He had extended his lines of communications beyond their limit, and he was now around 180 miles from his primary base of supply. Many of his men were without shoes, and he considered his army, in general, to be too ill-equipped and fatigued to enter so powerful a province as Virginia. After giving his men a rest period and allowing time for his wagons and stragglers to come up, he began a series of easy marches in the direction of Hillsborough.

The British general had allowed himself to be out-generalled and out-maneuvered in a campaign which even Tarleton admitted was "judiciously designed and vigorously executed." Greene's tactical superiority over Cornwallis in the first phase of the North Carolina campaign was demonstrated by one very evident fact—he won the race to the Dan.

CHAPTER VII
THE RECROSSING OF THE DAN

When Greene crossed the Dan he moved up to Halifax Court House in Virginia, fully expecting that Cornwallis would continue the pursuit across the river. All intelligence suggested such a course by the British, and the Americans were in no condition to fight. The general, despite his optimism at Guilford, was now convinced that he must not be brought to a decisive battle for he had become aware of the importance of his command. It had become apparent that so long as there was a Southern Army in the field to constitute a threat, hope would not die within the people, and there could be no rest for the British. The success of the American cause in the South rested upon the existence of that army.

Governor Thomas Jefferson was requested to call out the Virginia militia. He was also persuaded to grant Greene extralegal powers: "Take horses to mount your cavalry, and I will attempt to have it justified." It was only natural that a general who stressed mobility so much would take advantage of such a statement. Colonel Washington, although cautioned to act with "great delicacy," was allowed to seize horses to remount his troop. The colonel paid little attention to Greene's warning and confiscated even prize stallions in his quest for good mounts. He received a reprimand from Greene.

Inasmuch as all indications seemed to point to an early battle, Greene sent off dispatches to militia commanders soliciting early reinforcements. The general attempted to shame Governor Abner Nash of North Carolina into making greater efforts by boasting of Virginia's enthusiastic response to the call for men. To the North Carolina legislature he made an appeal that it complete its Continental quota of troops and reminded that body that every time it sent large groups of militia into the field it was but playing into the hands of the enemy.

As the Virginia militia poured in and with the report that Colonel John Campbell with 1,000 riflemen was on the march to join him, Greene felt that the time had come to renew the action, especially since the militia customarily remained in the field for such short periods. He planned an early recrossing of the Dan and entertained "hopes of giving Ld. Cornwallis a run in turn. At any rate, I shall attempt to gall his rear."

To observe and report the movements of the enemy, Lee's legion, two companies of Maryland Continental infantry, and the South Carolina militia were sent back across the river on February 18. The corps was to be under the command of Andrew Pickens, who was already on the far side of the Dan recruiting militia behind British lines. That night Greene, with a guard of dragoons, also recrossed the river to inform the group that their mission, in addition to reporting the activities of the enemy, was to intercept and harass British foraging parties and prevent the tories from rising. Just before daylight Greene left Pickens to rejoin his troops at Halifax Court House.

Upon his return there was the important intelligence that Cornwallis had left his camp and was on the march for Hillsborough. It was time for the hare to turn on the hounds.

When Greene had escaped over into Virginia, Cornwallis had not marched directly for Hillsborough; his men were too exhausted. Because of their fatigue he moved a short distance back from the river and allowed them a three days' rest. The rank and file, however, were not too weary to revert to their old habits of plundering, and the inhabitants were treated with such a lack of civility that the general used strong words condemning their actions in his general orders. The movement to Hillsborough was in a series of short marches. They arrived at Hillsborough on February 20. A proclamation was prepared, to be issued the following day when the Royal Standard was raised. But the ceremony was postponed until February 22 when the proclamation was made public and the standard raised to the accompaniment of a twenty-one gun salute. The proclamation called for all loyal subjects of the crown to repair immediately to Hillsborough, under arms and with enough provisions to last ten days. Royal Governor Martin busied himself with plans for the reestablishment of British government in North Carolina.

Despite the claims of royalist newspapers that loyalists were flocking to the Royal Standard and the proud boast that 700 had joined Lord Cornwallis in one day, little local strength was added to the British army. Many tories rode into Hillsborough to learn the news, inspect the king's troops and discuss the proclamation, but few expressed a desire to enter British service. Many harbored bitterness toward Britain because so few efforts had been made to assist them since the beginning of the war. Others voiced the opinion that the British army was spread out far too thin to offer security to their supporters. Some were dismayed at the ragged appearance of the troops. The slim response to his proclamation led Cornwallis to write of the North Carolina loyalists, "Our experience has shown that their numbers are not so great as had been represented and that their friendship was only passive."

To keep his men busy and out of mischief as well as to deprive them of an opportunity to plunder, Cornwallis directed that the village streets near his artillery park be paved. Stones were collected, and the intersection of King and Chewton streets was paved for 150 yards in all four directions. British soldiers, leaving the protection of the picket lines in search of whiskey, were often kidnapped or waylaid by rebels hanging about the fringes of the camp.

The supply situation became critical. The loyalists had not established the magazines that they had promised. The only cattle in the neighborhood were the oxen of the tories, and they were taken up and slaughtered despite the murmurings of their owners. Conditions worsened when a number of draft horses in the neighborhood were butchered to furnish the troops with fresh meat.

The whigs were growing bolder. A group of mounted militia under Major Joseph Graham, on its way to join Greene, heard that a detachment of twenty-nine soldiers was at Hart's Mill, a mile and a half from Hillsborough, used for grinding grain for the army. Graham divided his men into two groups, one party maneuvering in the open space before the mill while the remainder attacked from the rear. The British rank and file fled while their commanding officer, a young lieutenant, hid in the mill until the skirmish was over. Nine of the defenders were killed or wounded, and nineteen were taken prisoners. All were regulars except two tory militia. The gunfire alerted British patrols, and Graham was able to save his prisoners from recapture by splitting his command and leading the pursuers away from the group escorting the captives. Both groups reached Pickens's camp unharmed.

Prior to the arrival of Cornwallis in North Carolina the notorious tory partisan, Colonel David Fanning, had, without authority, published an advertisement promising a bounty of three guineas to each loyalist recruit, an assurance that he would not have to serve outside the two Carolinas and Georgia, plus a grant of land from the king at the end of the war. These enticements, coupled with Lord Cornwallis's proclamation, resulted in the embodiment of some 400 tories in the area between Deep and Haw rivers, under the leadership of a loyalist militia colonel, Doctor John Pyle. A request for protection was sent to Cornwallis, who notifed the tory colonel that Tarleton and his legion would meet them near the plantation of General John Butler. The loyalists made a picnic of their assembly, strolling about the neighborhood in a group, bidding their friends farewell, and drinking numerous toasts to each other and their cause.

Tarleton's departure from Hillsborough had not gone unnoticed, and he had been tailed by American patrols. When a scouting party reported that Cornwallis was still in town, Lee and Pickens decided to make a surprise attack upon Tarleton. As they trailed the British Legion, a farmer reported that the dragoon had made his midday stop just three miles ahead and was so confident of his safety that he had neglected to post pickets. In the vicinity of the legion camp the Americans formed a line and charged. There was no opposition. Tarleton had moved on. Two British staff officers who had remained behind to settle accounts with local loyalists were captured. Interrogation of the prisoners brought forth the information that the legion planned to camp at the plantation of Colonel William O'Neal, six miles ahead.

As they trotted along the road leading to O'Neal's, two armed men stepped from the roadside underbrush and hailed Pickens and Lee. During the subsequent conversation they indicated that they belong to Pyle's tories and had been sent to locate Tarleton who was to escort them to Hillsborough. They had mistaken the green tunics of Lee's legion for those of the British Legion. Pyle's group, they said, was in the road just ahead. Lee and Pickens, on the trail of bigger game, decided to bypass the loyalists and continue their pursuit of Tarleton. One of the tories, still under the impression that he had contacted Tarleton, and accompanied by two of Lee's dragoons, returned to Pyle with the request that the mounted troops be given the right of way as the troopers were weary and wished to make camp before nightfall. The militia were ordered to circle around through the dense woods on either side of the road.

The ruse almost succeeded. Pyle obligingly pulled his men to the side of the trail. Henry Lee, with a natural flair for military dramatics, carried the deception to the point of extending his hand to the tory colonel. The sounds of battle at the rear of the column discouraged further theatrics. The local mounted militia had been placed to the rear of the legion, their officers apparently uninformed of the scheme. A number of them, recognizing the red strips of cloth in the hats of the men alongside the road as the badge of toryism, began to murmur, fearful of their safety. To allay their fears, Captain Joseph Eggleston, an officer of Lee's legion who had been given the command of the mounted militia, rode up to one of the strangers who looked to be an officer and inquired as to his allegiance. When there was the proud answer, "To the King," Eggleston drew his sword and cut him across the head. His men, seeing the officer swing his sabre, rushed in.

"Light Horse Harry" Lee

The terrified tories, even after they were attacked, thought they were the victims of a horrible mistake, crying out, "You are attacking your own men!" "I am a friend of his Majesty!" and "Hurrah for King George!" One group of loyalists, determined to sell their lives as dearly as possible, banded together and began to fire wildly in all directions. Only one casualty resulted from their frenzied fire—a horse—as the legion cavalry rode them down.

Pyle's men scampered through the pines. Behind they left ninety of their number dead, and many of the survivors were wounded, including Colonel Pyle, who, according to tradition, hid in a small pond near the scene of the action until long after the fight was over. Lee and Pickens suffered the loss of only the one horse.

Soon after the action a band of Catawba Indians, fighting on the side of the Americans under Captain Oldham, came upon the scene and, before they could be controlled, killed seven or eight of the wounded tories by spear thrusts.

After assembling their scattered troops, Lee and Pickens marched to within three miles of Tarleton's camp and sent forward a party to observe his actions. They did not receive word of Tarleton's departure from O'Neal's plantation until an hour and a half after he pulled out. They pursued for a short distance. "This affair, however," Pickens reported to Greene, "has been of infinite service. It has knocked up Toryism altogether in this part."

The sounds of the massacre had not been heard by Tarleton. His first account of Pyle's defeat was after the arrival of several wounded loyalists who, still convinced that it had been Tarleton who had attacked them, complained bitterly of the cruelty of his dragoons. He prepared for an attack but decamped when a message from Cornwallis ordered him back to Hillsborough. Greene was reported to have recrossed the Dan and to be advancing on the British position.

Meanwhile, across the river in Virginia, Greene's army had been daily gathering strength. The militia had streamed in, 2,000 strong and another 1,000 reported on their way. The situation had seemed so promising that the general decided to move back across the river into North Carolina. Although supplies were still scarce, he felt that such a move would not only restore the confidence of the people, but would hamper British recruiting. As Greene explained his thinking, "It was best to put on a good face, and make the most of appearances."

The passage of the Dan was effected on February 23. Greene made a great display of strength and made a feint toward Hillsborough. The boldness of the rebels of late had magnified the size of his army in the eyes of Cornwallis's tory informants. It had been the reports of this supposedly mighty army that had led to the recall of Tarleton.

Hillsborough had become untenable for the British even before Greene came back across the river. The supply situation was such that Charles Stedman, the commissary, was forced to lead a party of men from house to house, requisitioning and confiscating provisions, regardless of the political affiliations of the owners.

On February 26, the day after the tory massacre, Cornwallis had led his army out of Hillsborough to a new position on Alamance Creek between the Deep and Haw rivers, a location promising a partial solution to the supply problem. This station could also give protection to the large number of loyalists in the area who had grown skittish after the Pyle affair.

The behavior of the troops continued to alienate and widen the breach between the local inhabitants and the military. Plundering continued unabated despite repeated warnings by the general. An investigation revealed that the women of the army were responsible for the more flagrant depredations. All campfollowers were ordered searched, and all articles they could not prove to be their personal property were burned. All women were required to attend frequent roll calls and, if found absent, were to be drummed out of camp. They were also required to witness all punishments.

There were other forces causing a rising tide of dissatisfaction among the loyalists. Tarleton's legion, on Deep River, had grown nervous and restless as a result of the hit and run tactics of American raiding parties who almost daily made a nuisance of themselves. A party of the more resolute tories, marching to offer their services to Cornwallis, were fired on by a jittery sentry. As they halted to consider their next course of action, the loyalists were charged by Tarleton's dragoons who had been alarmed by the shot. Those who were not cut down fled. As soon as the error was realized, a party of horsemen was sent out to round up the survivors, but they met with little success.

The following night, a patrol of Colonel Washington's cavalry ran across a band of twenty-five loyalists driving in cattle to the British army. In the engagement that followed, twenty-three of the herdsmen were killed.

Such small skirmishes, magnified to greater importance by Pyle's defeat, completely subdued the spirits of the loyalists in the district, and many of those who had come into the British army now slipped away to defend their homes against the whigs. So far, the British army's mission into North Carolina had failed, and there was now the need to bring Greene to a decisive battle and crush him to bolster the sagging morale of the loyalists. Cornwallis realized that he had to do something, even if it turned out to be wrong.

CHAPTER VIII

THE ROAD TO GUILFORD

Greene's army continued to gather strength. He kept the men on the move to gain the time necessary for the embodiment of the militia. The gains, however, were not consistent, with every skirmish resulting in a fluctuation of the returns. A considerable number of the newer troops and volunteers were under no obligations to remain very long in the field. Every wild shot by a high-strung picket was the signal for a reduction among the rank and file, "going home," said Greene, "to tell the news."

Yet the response of the North Carolina militia was greater than had been anticipated. Encouraging news came out of the west. There the backcountry mountain men, fighters by necessity, had refused to leave their homes exposed to the raids of the Cherokee and Chickasaw tribes, on the warpath as allies of the British. Since their defeat by the troops under the command of Colonel Arthur Campbell, the Indians were suing for peace. Greene, perhaps exceeding his powers, appointed Campbell as a commissioner to negotiate the treaty.

Little aid could be expected from the east. Major James Craig and his 400-man detachment had occupied Wilmington on February 1. With his coming the tories had come out of hiding, and the whigs had refused to "leave their Families exposed to a Set of Villains, who Dayley threatains their Destruction."

And provisions were somewhat easier to acquire, but the supply situation in the way of clothing and other articles had grown critical. In one letter Greene gently chided Governor Jefferson for sending such thinly-clad men into the field, their clothing so poorly made that it was falling to pieces; the padding was so thin that the shoulders of the men were rubbed raw by their muskets.

The division of his troops had functioned so well during the race to the Dan that Greene resorted to the same stratagem to guard against a surprise attack. Colonel Williams was once again placed in command of a light force and was issued orders to maneuver between the two armies as a buffer unit.

Foraging parties reported to Cornwallis that American patrols were operating in areas supposedly under the control of the British. Tarleton's entire corps was ordered into the sector. Small American units observed and reported his progress to Lee, who planned a surprise. Lee's legion had been reinforced by a large group of local militia and a few Catawba Indians. Near Clapp's Mill on Alamance Creek, he stationed his infantry behind a rail fence, their flanks protected by the mounted troops.

The unsuspecting Tarleton rode into the ambush. As soon as the confusion following the initial volley subsided, Tarleton pulled back to cover, formed a line of battle, and advanced on Lee's position. The Indians, with the first British volley, faded back through the trees. The British fire, as was customary, flew high but, through a curious twist of fate, was effective. The militia, experiencing combat for the first time, grew restless and uneasy as bark and leaves, cut from the trees by whining bullets, accentuated their fear. After a short period of desultory fire they began to stray toward the rear. Lee made an attempt to rally them, but just as soon as he halted one group and turned to another, the first resumed its withdrawal. Realizing that these men would never stand firm against a pressing action, and in view of the reports that the enemy were bringing up reinforcements, Lee thought it prudent to break off the engagement. The men were ordered to assemble in a defile to the rear. Dividing them into small detachments Lee sent them back to camp by different paths. There had been casualties. Although Tarleton admitted the loss of one officer and twenty rank and file killed and wounded, Lee's report to Greene stated that he had killed seven and wounded fifty of the enemy. Lee listed eight men killed and wounded.

As these intermediate groups were sparring, the two main armies drew off, each general waiting for the opposing general to show his hand. In the interim, representatives of the two forces met and arranged a prisoner exchange.

Cornwallis realized that Greene would not risk an action until he had been reinforced unless forced by British actions. Patrols came in with the word that Greene was still on the far side of Haw River, but his light troops were still occupying a position near the British army. Williams's command was described as split into smaller units and posted on small plantations to better facilitate subsistence. The general planned to attack these detachments, drive them back into the American army and then, if possible, invest Greene in a full scale battle. At 6:30 on the morning of March 6, the British army moved out toward Haw River.

That same morning Colonel Williams had planned to take advantage of an early morning fog to storm and seize the small British garrison stationed at a mill about a mile from his camp. The officer in charge rushed back into camp with the intelligence that Cornwallis had broken camp and even now was moving fast along a trail that would lead him into a position commanding Williams's left flank. He was within two miles of the light camp.

The American troops were put into motion, moving swiftly on the road leading to the ford at Weitzel's Mill on Reedy Fork Creek. Two enemy stragglers were brought in who volunteered the information that Weitzel's Mill was also the British objective and that Cornwallis planned to travel on a road paralleling Williams's path. Small flanking parties were dispatched to annoy the enemy column. They did little to slow enemy progress. The British vanguard, composed of Lieutenant Colonel Webster's brigade and Tarleton's dragoons, was pushing hard to intercept Williams before he reached the ford. The American rear guard often found itself on the flank rather than in front of the enemy. For almost ten miles the chase continued.

The pursuit became so hot that Colonel Williams found it necessary to form a party to provide covering fire as his troops crossed the stream. This unit was made up of the Virginia troops of Colonels John Preston and William Campbell, assisted by the militia of South Carolina and Georgia, all under Pickens's command. Cavalry from Lee's and Washington's troops were placed on the flanks.

This detachment threw a blistering fire into the advancing enemy, forcing them back in some disorder. By the time the British had reformed, Williams had managed to cross with the larger body of men which he formed on the far shore to furnish protective fire for the covering party. Cornwallis formed his men on the south bank of the Reedy Fork and sent forward a fording party under Colonel Webster. The British line was longer than that of the defenders and the flanks were able to deliver a murderous crossfire on the Americans. Cornwallis brought up his artillery as Webster's men, in the face of a heavy fire, splashed into the stream. The creek was not wide and they soon reached the far shore, although one British soldier later admitted it was "hot work."

The American right flank folded as the British gained a hill overlooking the defensive position. The militia ran. Williams was forced to issue orders to retreat, again forming a small party to cover the withdrawal. By ingenious ambushes they managed to so delay the pursuit of the enemy that after a mile they turned back to the creek. Major Ichabod Burnet, Greene's aide, galloped up with instructions for Williams to take a position on the north side of the Haw and keep the lines of communications open. That night they camped five miles from Weitzel's.

Both sides claimed light casualties. Tarleton declared that the Americans lost 100 men, killed and wounded, while British casualties numbered only thirty. On the other hand, the Americans listed small losses and claimed the enemy had lost around 100 men.

The greatest American loss was not in battlefield casualties but a sudden decrease in effective strength. The militia and back-country men of South Carolina and Georgia were nursing bruised feelings. They moped and muttered threats of going home, claiming they had been discriminated against and had been improperly exposed while covering the stream crossing of the regulars. Pickens consulted both Greene and Governor John Rutledge of South Carolina who was traveling with the Southern Army. Both advised Pickens to return home with the troops, with the general assuring him that he planned to return to the south just as soon as he could "break this fellow's [Cornwallis's] leg." Pickens was instructed to keep the enemy's force in South Carolina off balance through a series of nuisance raids.

The strength of those militia still with the army tended to fluctuate. Many volunteers had come in but finding army life disagreeable had taken a hasty leave. As Jefferson was to describe the situation, "they seem only to have visited and quitted him."

The action at Weitzel's Mill had indicated to Greene that his army was vulnerable to sudden attacks, and he was determined not to commit his troops to a battle until he had numerical superiority over the enemy. To gain the necessary time to realize this aim, he kept his army almost constantly on the move, seldom spending more than one night in the same bivouac. The country was ideal for such maneuvers. The dense semi-wilderness hindered British moves because of the possibility of ambush. Greene's own movements were unhindered by surplus equipment; he had brought few wagons back across the Dan and only enough tents to shelter the firearms in the event of a steady rain.

As Greene marched along the north bank of the Haw, Cornwallis maintained a parallel course on the opposite shore at a distance of some ten or twelve miles. On March 10, a large reinforcement of militia joined the American army at High Rock Ford on Haw River. Among these new arrivals were two brigades of North Carolina militia under Brigadier Generals John Butler and Thomas Eaton, a similar brigade from Virginia commanded by General Robert Lawson, and 400 Continental recruits from Maryland. The Southern Army was now sizable enough to command respect from the enemy, although the penchant of the militia to leave without permission could at any time reduce its strength.

Greene had arrived at the conclusion that only a sound drubbing would drive Cornwallis from the South, although he harbored doubts that his army was capable of administering such a defeat. Yet a battle, even a draw, would spirit up those people who were beginning to doubt the effectiveness of the Southern Army. And there was the possibility that a battle would so weaken the enemy that a subsequent engagement could result in victory. The morale of the army was high, and the talk around the campfires was of the coming battle. It was becoming clear, from the maneuvers of the British, that Cornwallis was attempting to gain a strategic advantage and force a battle. On March 12, Greene marched from High Rock Ford in the general direction of Guilford Court House.

Cornwallis, frustrated and restless, had come to feel that the salvation of his future lay in a defeat of Greene. He had allowed the American general to lure him away from possible security. He had instructed Major Craig to forward supplies up the Cape Fear River from Wilmington to Cross Creek, but the Americans were now in a position to intercept such supplies. A move toward Cross Creek would allow Greene to move on his rear at a time and place of his own choosing. Despite claims that the British army had suffered only 101 casualties on the march through North Carolina. Cornwallis's returns showed a loss of 227 men in the month of February alone—and there were those who declared that figure to be low.

When Greene moved up to Speedwell Iron Works on Troublesome Creek, eighteen miles from Guilford Court House, Cornwallis discovered himself to be at a disadvantage. With the fords of the Dan to the rear of the Americans offering them a route of withdrawal, there was no way to force them to fight. Yet he could not move too far from Greene to remedy his desperate supply situation

Charles, Lord Cornwallis

without leaving doubts in the minds of the loyalists as to the superiority of British arms.

To offer the tories one final opportunity to demonstrate their loyalty and to better feed his army, Cornwallis pitched camp on the plantation of William Rankin and Ralph Gorrel on North and South Buffalo creeks. His foraging parties were irritated by American patrols or partisan bands. He moved down to the Quaker Meeting House at New Garden between the forks of Deep River.

Both armies were ready and almost eager for battle. They had not long to wait.

CHAPTER IX

THE BATTLE OF GUILFORD COURT HOUSE

On March 14, 1781, British intelligence stated that Greene had received additional reinforcements and was expecting even more in the immediate future. During that afternoon, scouting parties reported that Greene had moved to Guilford Court House, just twelve miles from the British army, and had camped for the night. Cornwallis made his preparations for battle. His wagons and baggage were sent, under guard, to Bell's Mill on Deep River. At daybreak, March 15, the British column moved off toward Guilford.

The approach of the British army was reported to Greene, who sent Lee to feel out the strength of the enemy. The first contact came about four miles from New Garden when Lieutenant Heard of Lee's legion led Tarleton into a cleverly laid ambush. A sharp skirmish followed in which Lee seemed to be gaining the upper hand when Cornwallis sent forward the 23rd Regiment. With its appearance Lee wheeled his men and rode hard for the court house.

Greene had chosen this time to fight as he had reached the limit that he could expect in manpower. The time of a number of his militia was expiring, and he could expect but few replacements in the near future. He had nearly 4,400 men of whom 1,490 were Continentals; the British force was around 2,200.

Guilford Court House had been built on a hill which fell in a gradual slope for half a mile to the west, its toe dangling in a small creek. The ground was covered with a fairly dense growth of trees, spotted intermittently with old fields near the foot of the slope. Just above the stream, there were several large interconnecting fields. The area around the court house was cleared for about 400 yards. The road from Hillsborough to Salisbury bisected the battlefield. Near the court house this highway was joined by a secondary road leading to Reedy Fork Creek. On either edge of the area were irregularities in the ground that could serve as anchors for the flanks of defensive battle lines. Even as Greene positioned his troops, the sounds of the gun fire of the skirmish between Lee and Tarleton could be heard off in the distance.

Greene's deployment of troops was similar, although on a larger scale, to the arrangement of Morgan at Cowpens. This plan may well have been the result of a suggestion by Morgan, who had written Greene a short time earlier outlining his earlier disposition of troops.

Greene placed his men in three lines. The first was composed of the two brigades of North Carolina militia under Generals John Butler and Thomas Eaton. They were scattered along a rail fence that rambled along the skirt of the woods. Before them lay the open fields, affording an excellent field of fire. On the Salisbury road in the center two six-pounders under the command of Captain Anthony Singleton were positioned in such a fashion as to sweep all approaches. Inasmuch as this first line was made up of militia, Greene considered this to be his weakest, but Morgan had demonstrated their value as shock troops at Cowpens.

The second line was also militia, but they were Virginia militia and considered to be better than the average run of citizen soldiers. Many of the rank and file were ex-Continentals and a number of supernumerary Continental officers were in positions of responsibility. General Edward Stevens had been humiliated by the flight of the Virginia militia at the battle of Camden, and he was determined to prevent a repetition of their cowardice. Twenty paces to the rear of the second line he stationed twenty picked riflemen with orders to shoot the first man to quit his post. This second line was 300 yards to the rear of the first.

In the clearing around the court house, 400 yards to the rear of the Virginia militia, Greene positioned his third line composed of his crack troops, the Continentals. They were stationed on a hill overlooking a shallow ravine. Seeking the advantage of the contour of the rise to command the open fields, these men were drawn up in double formation. The right front was made up of the Fourth and Fifth Virginia Continentals under Colonel John Green and Lieutenant Colonel Samuel Hawes; the two units were commanded by Brigadier General Isaac Huger. The two Maryland regiments, the First and Second, of Colonel John Gunby and Lieutenant Colonel Benjamin Ford, were on the left and commanded by Colonel Otho Williams. The two remaining cannons directed by Captain John Finley squatted between the two fronts. The only veteran troops were those of Gunby; Ford's Second Regiment had but recently joined the Southern Army. Their strength lay in their officers who were all battle-tested. Greene held no force in reserve, for he was aware of the British strength and knew that Cornwallis would have to commit his entire command to prevent being outflanked.

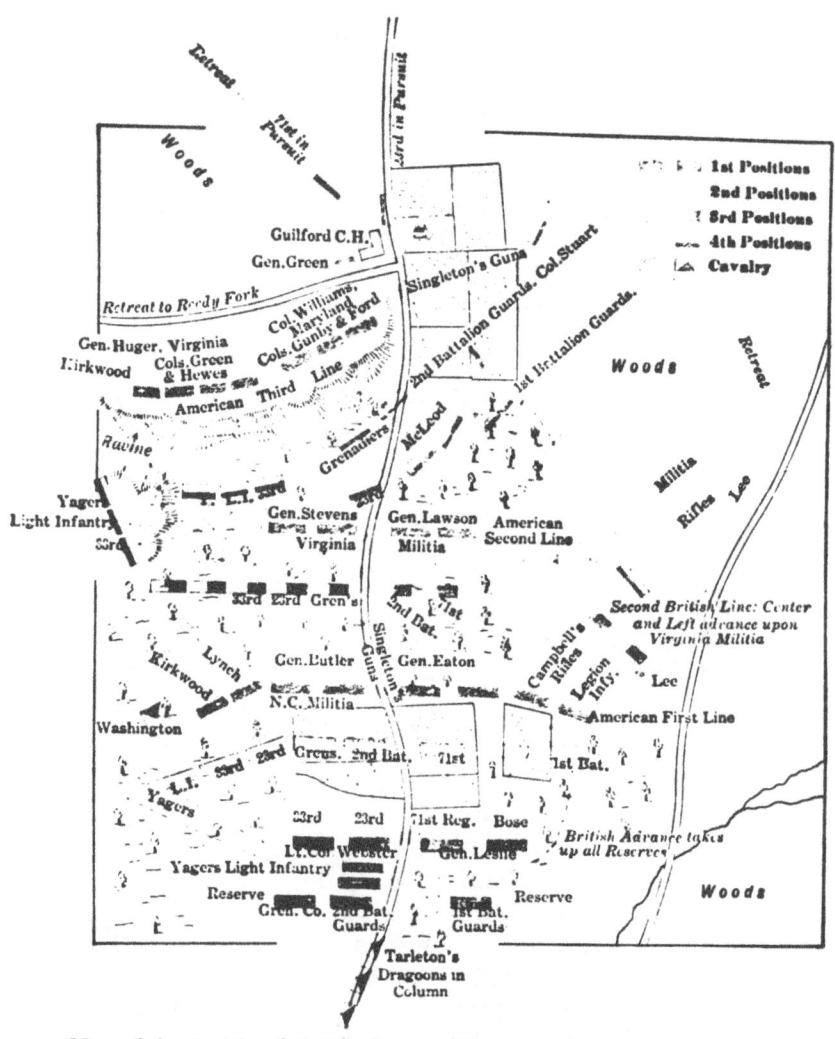

Map of the Battle of Guilford Court House, drawn by Lt. Joseph A. Baer of the U.S. Military Academy. Map Collection, Division of Archives and History.

As security for the right flank, there were Washington's dragoons, a light infantry detachment, and a regiment of riflemen under Colonel Charles Lynch, all slightly to the rear of the third line. Lee's legion of seventy-five cavalry and eighty-two infantry was on the left. A short distance behind the legion were the 200 Virginia riflemen of Colonel William Campbell.

Greene then rode along his front line, promising the uneasy militiamen that if they would but give the enemy two good volleys they could retire from the field. Then, in his dry Rhode Island twang, he reminded them that they were fighting for liberty and that they should prove themselves worthy of the cause. But it remained for the ebullient Henry Lee, a man who could almost strut on horseback, to fire their enthusiasm. He rode along the entire front of the army, telling them to stand firm and not fear the British. He swore loudly that he had already whipped the enemy that morning and could do it again.

It was around 1:30 that afternoon when the British first came into view. Cornwallis surveyed the field. The dense woods made an extensive use of mounted troops impracticable. Artillery could be moved forward only along the road, and this would be contested by Singleton's guns and the enfilading fire from the first line. On the left the trees were not so thick, and the British general decided to concentrate his efforts in that sector.

As the redcoats moved forward for deployment, Singleton's two six-pounders began to bark. Cornwallis brought up his own artillery to return the fire. As the men wheeled into line, Lieutenant Henry O'Hara, of the Royal Artillery, was killed by sniper fire. The North Carolina militia stared as the British regulars quick-stepped into their formation.

The right front line was composed of the Hessian Regiment du Bose and the British 71st Regiment, supported by the first battalion of Guards, all under the command of Major General Alexander Leslie. On the left were the 23rd and 33rd regiments under Colonel Webster. They were supported by the Grenadiers and second battalion of Guards, with the left front under the direction of Brigadier General Charles O'Hara. The light infantry of the Guards, along with the Hessian jaegers were in the trees to the left of the artillery. The cavalry remained in the road, out of range of enemy fire, to be used as circumstances dictated.

The fields, recently ploughed, were muddy from the late rains. The line moved forward at a steady pace. They were met by a "most galling and destructive fire," and a captain of the 71st Regiment later declared that half his men "dropt on the spot." Forty yards from the rail fence the attacking force could see the ugly black muzzles of muskets, seemingly in their very faces. The red line paused, wavered, and appeared on the verge of breaking, but were quickly steadied by the shouts of Colonel Webster. He ordered a volley, to be followed by a charge.

The long line of bright steel reminded the militia they had no bayonets with which to parry the thrusts of the enemy. They fled, in their terror throwing away arms, cartouche boxes, and all equipment they felt to be an encumbrance. Eaton, Butler, and William R. Davie all attempted to stem the tide. Lee galloped among them, shouting threats that he would charge them with his cavalry. They still ran. Singleton's guns were hurriedly wheeled back to the third line and placed on the left flank. The militia, in their flight, obliqued toward the flanks, leaving the British exposed to the fire of the second line.

The second line stood steady. General Stevens had warned his troops that the first line would probably fold before the British advance and had instructed them to open ranks to allow the fugitives to flow through to the rear.

The fire from the second line and the flanking parties was so severe that Cornwallis was compelled to bring up his reserves and change his front. The first battalion of Guards was brought up to strengthen the right wing and, accompanied by the Regiment du Bose, obliqued toward the right flank where Lee's cavalry and Campbell's riflemen waited. The jaegers and light infantry came in on the left to drive against Washington and Lynch. Tarleton's dragoons remained as the only reserve, and they sat watching the battle.

With this additional manpower strengthening his flanks, Webster drove forward against the Virginians. The dense woods not only prevented the maintenance of an orderly line but hampered a bayonet charge. There was a tendency for the battle to break up into a series of small, scattered skirmishes.

The American second line held on with such tenacity that Tarleton was to declare, "at this period the event of the action was doubtful, and victory alternately presided over each army." General Stevens took a musket ball through the thigh and had to be helped from the field. Still the majority of his men stood stubborn until the sheer force of numbers forced them into an orderly withdrawal. They had also been weakened when one of their regiments fled in panic when they discovered enemy units in their rear. Cornwallis personally led the charge that finally broke the resistance of the Virginians, having his horse shot beneath him as he spurred forward.

With the second line no longer a problem, the first battalion of Guards was the first group to break into the cleared area around the court house. The brave, but overzealous Webster, without hesitating long enough to allow supporting troops to come up, charged the First Maryland Regiment. Gunby's men drove back the British with a withering fire. Webster fell back to await reinforcements. The British colonel had received a musket ball through the knee, a wound that was to prove fatal within a fortnight. Greene rode along the American line, calling upon them to stand firm and deliver a killing blow to the enemy when they returned to the attack.

General O'Hara brought up the second battalion of Guards under Lieutenant Colonel Charles Stuart to strengthen Webster. The artillery was manhandled up the road to a small knoll near the woods, allowing them a field of fire commanding the American position in supporting the assault troops.

Stuart led his men forward in a charge against the raw recruits of Ford's Second Maryland who were experiencing combat for the first time. As the red line surged forward, the Marylanders broke. Singleton's six-pounders were quickly overrun and captured.

Gunby ordered a counter charge by the First Maryland. As he shouted the command, his horse was killed, pinning the body of its rider to the ground. The command fell to Lieutenant Colonel Howard. Howard immediately wheeled the regiment so as to intercept the left flank of the Guards. After pouring in a fire at short range, they pushed forward with the bayonet.

Colonel Washington, who had been forced to fall back with the second line, was ordered to charge with his dragoons. The British attack disintegrated before this unexpected stroke and, thrown into confusion, began to fall back toward the protection of their artillery. The captured guns were retaken by the Americans. Cornwallis, sensing a rout, attempted to rally his troops. Failing to halt the retreat, he galloped over to the artillery and ordered a charge of grape shot to be fired at Washington's cavalry, although the retreating Guards were in the direct line of fire. General O'Hara, who had been wounded, strongly protested the order, but Cornwallis insisted that his orders be carried out. Many of the Guards dropped, killed by their own artillery. But the Americans had been stopped, and the 23rd and 71st regiments had been given the time to come forward in support.

The appearance of these fresh troops, plus the support of the artillery, persuaded Howard and Washington to fall back on their original positions as once again the enemy pressed forward. Singleton's two guns were once again taken as were Finley's artillery that had been placed with the third line. The flight of the Second Maryland had so weakened the left side of the American position that the flank was soon turned, and there were reports that British troops had gotten to the rear of the Virginia Continentals. The right flank was in danger of folding. The artillery had been abandoned because the draft horses had been killed, and the fierceness of the battle had prevented their removal by manpower. In general, the American forces had been scattered and there was no definite line of resistance.

Greene decided a strategic withdrawal to be his best course of action. He designated the Virginia Continentals under Huger to be the rear guard. The retreat was orderly and well conducted. The 23rd and 71st regiments were ordered to pursue but were recalled when Cornwallis learned the extent of his casualties.

The battle still raged over on the fringes of the right flank where Lee and Campbell were engaged by the Regiment du Bose and the first battalion of Guards under General Leslie. The legion and Campbell's riflemen had been difficult to dislodge and had taken a heavy toll among the enemy. Units had become separated, and the thick undergrowth discouraged the use of the bayonet. The riflemen would hide among the thickets until an enemy unit had passed and then pour in a heavy fire upon their rear.

These Americans were slowly pushed back to the summit of a small hill where they attempted to make a stand. The Guards made their way up the slope to form a covering fire for the Regiment du Bose who drove off the defenders. As the weary British troops halted to await further orders, a small group of American riflemen slipped in behind them and from the cover of the trees delivered an annoying fire at long range. Cornwallis dispatched Tarleton to investigate. Under a covering fire by the Regiment du Bose, the dragoons charged and flushed the riflemen from the trees. They circled around to follow the Salisbury road until they found the side road leading to the rendezvous at Speedwell Iron Works.

So ended the battle of Guilford Court House, an engagement lasting but an hour and a half, but whose effects were to be felt at Yorktown.

Greene retreated approximately three miles across Reedy Fork Creek. There he halted to allow the stragglers to catch up. Rain had begun to fall and the march was slow. It was near daylight on March 16 when they trudged into the camp at the Iron Works.

Greene was physically exhausted, but he cast aside his fatigue to direct defensive preparations, for he fully expected Cornwallis to follow up the battle with another blow. Earthworks were thrown up on the bluffs overlooking Troublesome Creek. Morale was high, and the men talked of a second action with no fear in their voices. Greene had not removed his clothes or enjoyed the comfort of a bed for the past six weeks; that night he fainted; he collapsed again the following night.

As he awaited the next move of the British, Greene surveyed his own situation. His losses amounted to 1,255 men, but many of these were listed as missing. Of this total, 576 were charged to the fleet-footed North Carolina militia, who had lost only seven killed and six wounded; the remaining 563 were missing. The greatest loss had been the 290 casualties among the Continentals. He had also lost his four artillery pieces. Still, he had not lost his sense of humor, especially after he heard British losses, for it was later reported that a message to Cornwallis offered him "four more cannon on the same terms if he would accept them."

But now that the great battle was over, Greene's army was shrinking. Although a few militia still drifted in, others were leaving daily "to return home to kiss their wives and sweethearts." The Virginia militia had come out for six weeks, but a number were leaving before their time was up.

Greene, ambitious and conscious of his place in history, sought to fix the blame for his defeat and settled upon the North Carolina militia, declaring that at least half of them had fled without firing a shot. His irritation was so evident, and his criticism so caustic that his friend Joseph Reed, president of the Pennsylvania Executive Council, cautioned him not to express so openly his contempt for the militia, nor should he attribute all of his failures in the South to them. An attitude of superiority by the Continental officers, he said, would be resented and alienate the "bulk of the country." He suggested that Greene adopt the same attitude toward the militia as one should toward a wife:

> Be to their faults a little blind,
> And to their virtues very kind.

Three days were spent at Speedwell Iron Works, just waiting. Word came that Cornwallis was withdrawing toward the Yadkin River; a little later more reliable intelligence reported his destination as Bell's Mill. Greene issued marching orders.

Since the end of the battle, the uninjured troops of Cornwallis had been caring for the wounded of both armies who lay scattered over a large area. British soldiers were without either tents or provisions and were dead tired as a result of their early rising, the march, and the subsequent battle on March 15. Despite their fatigue they had been put to work caring for the wounded and burying the dead. A downpour that night drowned the sighs of the wounded and the groans of the dying; it was estimated that at least fifty men alone died in the rain that night. The wagons from Bell's Mill with the baggage and medical supplies did not arrive on the scene until between three and four o'clock during the afternoon of March 16. Their arrival did little to alleviate the sufferings of the men; each was issued a pound of flour and a small quantity of lean beef. Dent's Mill, a grist mill in the neighborhood, furnished some flour but its machinery was soon worn out from continuous use. The desperate situation gave truth to the words of Charles Stedman, "Here, time, place, and numbers, all united against the British."

At eight o'clock on the morning of March 17, seventeen wagons loaded with wounded left Guilford Court House, jolting over the rough road back to New Garden Meeting House. Later in the day the women of the army were sent off along the same route.

British casualties had been heavy: 93 killed, 413 wounded, and 26 missing. There was no way that Cornwallis could estimate Greene's losses. Few prisoners had been taken, as the thick woods had facilitated their escape. His foraging parties, however, came in with the reports that the houses in the surrounding countryside were crowded with rebel wounded. The British had captured 4 brass six-pounders, 180 round shot, and 50 case shot, along with 2 ammunition wagons. They had also taken 1,300 small bore weapons, some of which were distributed among the local loyalists; others were destroyed in the field.

Cornwallis remained at Guilford until noon, Monday, March 18, burying the dead, nursing the wounded, and making plans for a march to the coast. Because of the unknown strength of Greene's army and the barrenness of the area, he planned to move to Cross Creek in a series of easy marches.

He received little support from local loyalists. Yet, assuming the posture of the conqueror before leaving, Cornwallis issued a proclamation claiming a "compleat victory" and inviting all good loyalists to join the forces of the crown. His last act before leaving was to burn the house of a Mr. Campbell, a prominent whig of the community. Then he marched.

Guilford Court House had been a vicious and bitterly contested engagement in which the fortunes of war had determined the victor, although Greene claimed the outcome to be the result of superior British discipline. Both commanding generals had displayed great personal courage, and each had been in danger of capture by the enemy. Cornwallis had two horses killed beneath him and had been slightly wounded but had refused to allow his name to be included in the casualty list. The ferocity of the battle had so awed the British general that later he reportedly said, "I never saw such fighting since God made me. The Americans fought like demons."

In New York and Charleston loyalists held jubilant celebrations when they heard of Cornwallis's claims to victory. In England opinion was divided along political affiliations. The *London Magazine* declared Guilford Court House to be the most glorious victory yet won by the king's forces in America and forecast an early return to royal allegiance by the people of North Carolina and Virginia. The staid *Annual Register*, however, solemnly proclaimed, "That victory . . . was productive of all the consequences of defeat." Horace Walpole, still nursing his dislike of Cornwallis, condemned the general with, "Lord Cornwallis has conquered his troops out of shoes and provisions, and himself out of troops," and predicted that such victories left little hope for ultimate British success.

Charles James Fox, bitter opponent of the government in power, cried out that, "Another such victory would be the ruin of the British Army." One observer, noting that the government made little of the claims of victory, wrote, "as headquarters rather commends than vaunts, I guess the glory of the day was greater than the utility."

And even for Cornwallis, the claim of "victory" held a hollow ring.

CHAPTER X
THE HARE TURNS ON THE HOUND

The wagons and campfollowers were awaiting Cornwallis at New Garden Meeting House. A number of his wounded were in no condition for additional travel. At least seventy of his men, and perhaps thirty American wounded, were left in the improvised hospital in the Meeting House, with Cornwallis confident that the gentle Quakers of the community would not allow them to go unattended.

On March 19, the shattered army arrived at Bell's Mill, where the general allowed his weary men a two-day rest and took the opportunity to collect a small supply of provisions. He still hoped to recruit loyalists, but the bedraggled appearance of the troops dampened enthusiasm for British service. Many of the inhabitants rode into camp, shook the hand of the British general, told him that they were glad he had whipped Greene, and then rode home again. When he left Bell's Mill, Cornwallis directed his march toward Cross Creek where he hoped to find plentiful supplies, sent up from Wilmington by Major Craig. The many walking wounded dictated a succession of short marches.

Greene began the pursuit. When he received reliable intelligence that Cornwallis had left Guilford, he broke camp on Troublesome Creek. He left his wounded at the court house, later requesting the Quakers at New Garden to care for his men, reminding them that he, too, had once been a member of their faith.

Lee was sent forward to gather intelligence and to demonstrate to the local people that the American army had not been destroyed. The legion was to range off the British flanks. The straggling march of the British column allowed a number of prisoners to be taken each day.

Lee sent back word that Cornwallis had halted for a few days at Ramsey's Mill on Deep River to comfort his wounded and to gather provisions. His men had been set to work building a bridge across the river as a means of getting the wounded across. Greene had also been forced to slow his pursuit, awaiting provisions and ammunition. Lee was ordered to cross the river ten miles above the British bivouac and make his way down the opposite bank. He was to dislodge the British bridgehead, destroy the bridge, and deny passage of the stream to Cornwallis until Greene could come up from the rear. Cornwallis learned of the scheme, decamped, crossed the stream, and moved as rapidly as possible toward Cross Creek. His departure was so sudden that he left several of his men, who had but recently died of their wounds, unburied on the site. Lee arrived in time to prevent the destruction of the bridge by the rear guard.

Greene reached Ramsey's Mill the following day. He decided to discontinue the pursuit. The militia were daily leaving, and there was little hope of gaining any replacements in the "vile toryish country from Hillsborough to Cape Fear." The pine barrens on the road to Cross Creek promised little in the way of subsistence, especially after the enemy had made their way along that path.

Cross Creek held many promises for the British army. The Scottish Highlanders of the area were predominantly tory and reportedly were anxious to take up arms on the side of the crown. But there was nothing but disappointment facing Cornwallis. The inhabitants proved timid and allergic to army life. The Cape Fear had proved unsatisfactory as a supply route, as shipments up the river had been waylaid by the whigs living on either side of the stream. There were few provisions, and a search revealed that there was only four days' forage within twenty miles of Cross Creek. There was also smallpox in the town. On April 1, 1781, Cornwallis marched for Wilmington.

The British column that struggled along the coastal plain of North Carolina bore little of the proud martial appearance it had presented when it left South Carolina three months earlier. The British resembled more a gaggle of refugees from a comic opera. Uniforms that had flashed with bright colors were now dirty, faded, and torn. Behind the limping column came the camp-followers, the women riding side saddle on fine horses and bedecked in elegant dresses and petticoats that had but recently hung in the closet of some planter's wife. These "harpies" were feared more than the soldiers and were ruthless in stripping rings from the fingers of their owners, while children were choked in front of their parents to force them to reveal where the valuables were concealed.

There was some local retailiation. The militia of Bladen County, led by General Alexander Lillington, harassed the rear of the enemy column so effectively that by the time Cornwallis reached the coast his losses had increased by an additional thirteen men killed with another fifteen or twenty wounded. British stragglers were often attacked by a motley troop under the leadership of Baron du Glaubeck whom Greene had recently appointed commander of the North Carolina militia cavalry—if he could raise them. Upon assembling his command, Glaubeck discovered only one man had a sword. Undaunted, he armed his men with cudgels and attacked the enemy whenever an opportunity presented itself.

At Wilmington, despite reports that Greene's army was threatening British posts in South Carolina, Cornwallis decided to follow through with his original objective—the subjugation of Virginia. General Clinton had earlier sent Major General William Phillips into Virginia with orders to create a diversion and to cooperate with Cornwallis. Cornwallis reasoned that if he could make a junction with Phillips it could mean instant reinforcements. To return to South Carolina would be a tacit admission of defeat. On April 24 he marched for Virginia, declaring that he was "quite tired of marching about the Country in Quest of Adventure."

Greene had remained at Ramsey's Mill for several days, resting his troops and working on a plan for future actions. He realized that it was imperative that he move out of this semi-wilderness. Almost daily men were dropping from malnutrition. The people of the region were of divided allegiances and had drifted into a vicious little civil war that threatened to "depopulate this part of the country."

He came up with a fluid plan of operations, based on his return to South Carolina. There he hoped to intercept enemy lines of communications and isolate the posts stretching across the state. This move, he hoped, would force Cornwallis to return southward. He also felt that the return of the American army would bolster the sagging spirits of the people of South Carolina who had begun to feel that they were being neglected. A return to the south would benefit the people of North Carolina as it would give them a respite from the ravages of war and foraging armies and, hopefully, would allow the legislature to recruit its quota of Continental troops. On April 6, Greene set out upon the return march to South Carolina.

The beginning of his march marked the end of the contest between Greene and Cornwallis. It had been a disastrous campaign for the British general, despite all of his claims of victory.

He had been outgeneralled and outmaneuvered. Cowpens, Guilford, and the skirmishes framing the larger battles were all contributing factors of eventual defeat, perhaps best explained by Greene's rather wistful reply when he heard of Washington's investment of Cornwallis at Yorktown, "We have been beating the bush, and the General has come to catch the bird."

So rashly and with such a lack of foresight had Cornwallis conducted his campaign that a later British historian was led to conclude that the "mad invasion of North Carolina" was the result of a nervous breakdown caused by worry and strain. His invasion had resembled a boat ploughing through a stream, with the bow pushing aside the water which then closes in behind the stern. Perhaps Joseph Reed best summed up the campaign:

> like a desolating meteor he had passed, carrying destruction and distress to individuals—his army has walked through the country, daily adding to the number of its enemies, and leaving their few friends exposed to every punishment for their ill-timed and ill-placed confidence.

Greene had not always taken full advantage of his opportunities, but he had usually realized his shortcomings. He had searched for glory and had lost. Evaluating his efforts, he declared: "Here has been the field for the exercise of genius, and an opportunity to practice all the great and little acts of war. Fortunately we have blundered through without meeting with capital misfortune."

Greene had indeed blundered, but his mistakes had been offset by his practice of anticipating eventualities. He made a science of retreat, and, inveterate planner that he was, his plotting of retrograde movements suggested greater genius than those moments when he strove for victory. He was respected as a worthy foe, and his ability to strike, fall back, and strike again was perhaps summed up in his own words, "We Fight, Get Beat, Rise and Fight Again." Appreciation of his talents was expressed in the observations of a British officer serving to the north who wrote in his diary:

> Greene is however entitled to great praise for his wonderful exertions; the more he is beaten, the farther he advances in the end. He has been indefatigable in collecting troops and leading them to be defeated.

Perhaps the greatest weakness of British strategy was that their generals insisted upon European battlefield tactics in a terrain that bore little resemblance to the more open European countryside. More observant Englishmen had foreseen the result of British military practices when one wrote, in 1775, "our army will be destroyed by damned driblets . . . America is an ugly job . . . a damned affair indeed." And by 1781 the *Annual Register* pointed out:

> Most of these actions would in other wars be considered as skirmishes of little account, and scarcely worthy of a detailed narrative. But these small actions are as capable of any of displaying military conduct. The operations of war being spread over that vast continent, by the new plan that was adopted, it is by such skirmishes that the fate of America must be necessarily decided. They are therefore as important as battles in which a hundred thousand are drawn up on each side.

For Cornwallis, the campaign of 1781 in the Carolinas had been a study in frustration, with the British general desperately attempting to strike a decisive blow that would eliminate the Southern Army, and with Greene seeking that ever-elusive victory that would bring him glory and his place in history.

And as contemporary doggerel would have the campaign, sung to the tune of "Yankee Doodle":

> Cornwallis led a country dance,
> The like was never seen, sir;
> Much retrograde and much advance,
> And all with General Greene, sir.
> They rambled up and rambled down
> Joined hands and off they ran, sir;
> Our General Greene to old Charlestown
> And the Earl to Wilmington, sir.

Suggestions for Further Reading

A documented copy of my M.A. thesis, from which this is taken, is on deposit in the Library of the University of North Carolina at Chapel Hill.

Books which are concerned with the subject include: M. F. Treacy, *Prelude to Yorktown: The Southern Campaign of Nathanael Greene, 1780-1781* (Chapel Hill: University of North Carolina Press, 1963); Don Higginbotham, *Daniel Morgan: Revolutionary Rifleman* (Chapel Hill: University of North Carolina Press, 1961); Theodore Thayer, *Nathanael Greene: Strategist of the American Revolution* (New York: Twayne Publishers, 1960); and Franklin and Mary Wickwire, *Cornwallis: The American Adventure* (Boston: Houghton Mifflin Company, 1970). Many of Greene's letters are included in the old biographical study by his grandson, George Washington Greene, *The Life of Nathanael Greene: Major-General in the Revolution* (New York: Hurd and Houghton, 3 vols., 1867-1871).

ABOUT THE AUTHOR

Hugh Franklin Rankin was born in Virginia and reared in Reidsville, North Carolina. He received his bachelor's degree at Elon College before earning his M.A. and Ph.D. degrees at the University of North Carolina, Chapel Hill. Having taught at Tulane University in New Orleans, Louisiana, since 1957, he was appointed W. R. Irby Professor of History in 1974. Professor Rankin is the author of a distinguished list of books, articles, and pamphlets, including *The Golden Age of Piracy* (Williamsburg, 1969); *The North Carolina Continentals* (Chapel Hill, 1971); and *Francis Marion: The Swamp Fox* (New York, 1973).

CPSIA information can be obtained
at www.ICGtesting.com
Printed in the USA
LVHW102345221122
733827LV00003B/26